MAXIMISING YOUR INCOME

AS A MODERN DAY SPORTS COACH

Adam Lambe

© 2021 Adam Lambe

All rights reserved. No part of this publication may be reproduced, distributed, or transmitted in any form or by any means, including photocopying, recording, or other electronic or mechanical methods, without the prior written permission of the publisher, except in the case of brief quotations embodied in critical reviews and certain other noncommercial uses permitted by copyright law. For permission requests, please write to: adam@themarketingnet.ch

ISBN Paperback: 978-1-3999-0392-9
ISBN eBook: 978-1-3999-0393-6

Cover image: Adobe Stock/vipman4
Cover and inner design by Andy at meadencreative.com

CONTENTS

Foreword	1
Introduction: Lessons learnt through failure	3
Important – Professional Code of Conduct	7
1 Self Development & Creating the Vision	11
2 The Ever-Changing Coaching Landscape	23
3 Change Your Bread & Butter Coaching (Everyday Coaching)	33
4 Product Sales & Service Commissions – The Next Gear to Higher Earnings	59
5 Customer Acquisition & Retention	75
6 Must-Have Communication Tools	89
7 Building Business & Successful Partnerships	113
8 Generating Income Online	131
9 Become a Key Person of Influence	159
10 Money Matters	177
Conclusion	187

FOREWORD

You're a sports coach: What comes up if I were to Google your name? Anything? Nothing? Blogs, videos, a website? Positive or negative reviews? In this day and age you are who Google says you are. If you're not visible, or if Google spits out some negative information about you, you are going to struggle to make a successful career. Like it or lump it, the successful Modern Day Sports Coach needs to embrace a lot of new ideas. And you need to be known, liked and trusted to get ahead. You will, rightly or wrongly, be compared to other coaches in your profession on YouTube and other social media platforms.

However, if you're passionate about what you deliver, you stand out as offering a remarkable service and/or products, and you can articulate that online, the digital age can propel you to fame and fortune before you can say "Sorry Mrs. Smith my agenda is full until next April". So how do you "Get the knowledge" to succeed as a Modern Day Sports Coach? Needless to say, the information lies in the wisdom and experience in the following chapters.

In this book, Adam shares with you his Golden Nuggets for the "Digital Age" in how to maximize your coaching income - some old tried and trusted methods, some experimental, and some aimed at this rapidly changing coaching environment. The magic lies in aligning the Nuggets within, to your own coaching strategy and demographic.

I am almost solely responsible for bringing Adam into golf as his first Golf Coach back in 1995 at Newquay Golf Club in Cornwall, UK. Since day 1, he was a sponge for knowledge both as a player and, since 2002 as a PGA coach. This quest for knowledge has never ceased. And now, combining his considerable experience as a PGA Professional at 3 prestigious Clubs in Spain, Switzerland and Germany, and his expertise as a qualified Digital Marketing Consultant, he pens concisely his knowledge and wisdom into this book.

Andrew Cullen, PGA Golf Professional

INTRODUCTION
LESSONS LEARNT
THROUGH FAILURE

Since I started coaching almost 20 years ago, much has changed. The modern sports coach requires unique skills in order to thrive in today's environment. Marketing and Social Media, Advertising and Sponsorship, Products and Sales, Technology and Finance are only some of the skills required today to maximise your potential income as a contemporary sports professional. The days of simply turning up to a full coaching agenda are all but gone, and a full-time income based purely on coaching is becoming more and more difficult to attain.

This book is intended to help you understand all the potential ways you have to maximise your income as a sports coach and set you on the road to high earnings and financial freedom. There is 20 years of experience in this book, as well as my own positive and negative life lessons. I started my coaching career in debt. However, step by step, through many mistakes and failures I have dug myself out of the negative cycle. All the tips and advice listed here are tried and tested, either by myself or by fellow coaches who have implemented them with great success.

I will share my thoughts and opinions on the all the potential sources of income across the entire of spectrum of the coaching environment: not only will these ideas increase your income but they will also help you to establish yourself as a key person of influence within your region. Life is one big journey of learning and development, and I certainly still have lots to learn and mistakes to make. I hope through this book you will be able to avoid some of the pitfalls I encountered along the way, and move quickly and confidently towards financial freedom. My goal is to give you all the knowledge you need to build a successful sustainable coaching business and to find the road to long term happiness.

I am a PGA Golf Professional and many of the topics and ideas in this book are based on the golf Industry, however I am confident that coaches from all sports can implement the ideas within this book successfully in their businesses.

When I became a Golf Professional back in 2002, I was young, charismatic, confident and ready to take on the world. I had landed a six-month contract with a great salary at a golf club in Switzerland and I was on my way up. I had been working in the UK with my Dad on a building site to save a little money for my epic journey into mainland Europe. Seven months later, I was bankrupt, unhappy and facing the horrible prospect of returning to the UK with my tail between my legs!

Fast forward to 2020 and I am still living in Switzerland, the head professional of my local golf club and the owner of multiple businesses, assets and properties. I consistently generate more income year on year, I am a sports ambassador for a luxury sports car brand, and a Swiss watch company. I have coaching partnerships and distribution contracts with successful businesses, I have my own YouTube channel, I hold seminars for coaches and I have published a book.

So what changed between 2002 and 2020?

In this book I will take you through all the important lessons I have learnt over that period and give you the absolute blueprint on how to build a successful, sustainable coaching business, and to maximise your income.

I hope this book will open your eyes to the potential you have inside you, and help you realise the value you can give your customers: and that, if you are willing to find smart ways to work diligently, there is no limit to your abilities and your income.

"The more you invest in your own knowledge, your own skills, and the relationships you build with other people, the more success you will have. Share your wisdom with the intention to help others and you will reap the rewards"

Adam Lambe

IMPORTANT – PROFESSIONAL CODE OF CONDUCT

This book is intended to help you increase your reputation as a sports coach, charge a premium for your services and increase your earnings through multiple channels. It is important to mention that nothing included in this book is intended to teach you to *mislead* or *take advantage* of your customers: quite the opposite. The ideas here will instead improve and strengthen the relationships you have with your target audience.

As you offer more and more interesting services and add enormous value to them, your customers will gravitate more towards you and trust in your recommendations and opinions. I have added sections on self-development and finance only as a way to share my beliefs and blueprint with you. I am not a qualified financial advisor or a spiritual guide, but I have read hundreds of books on business, self development, entrepreneurship and coaching. And through this knowledge I have learnt that the more respectful and genuine we are as coaches the more successful we become.

Build all the systems in this book with the intention of providing your customers with excellent service and value and treat all those who cross your path with the same respect as you wish to be treated.

CUSTOMER VS. CLIENT

I use the term "customer" in this book to describe any person who may want to purchase your products or services. I am well aware that many coaches will regard their audience as "clients" rather than "customers". For the sake of the simplicity of this book and the many products and services we hope to sell in order to maximise our income the term "customer" is more appropriate.

LAYOUT

The book is divided up into chapters which help you navigate through it more easily: each section has valuable information on how you can increase your income and build a successful business.

Each section can be read separately, but I would recommend reading through the entire book from start to finish in order to build your successful coaching business.

At first you may be overwhelmed by all the information and feel like it would take an eternity to implement it all, but if you take small consistent steps forward you will see that you can achieve a lot in a short period of time. At the end of each chapter there is a small summary which highlights the most important points and the key takeaways.

MAXIMISING YOUR INCOME

1
SELF DEVELOPMENT & CREATING THE VISION

The biggest investment you can make in the success of your business is actually in yourself. Investing in yourself physically, mentally and spiritually will give you the energy drive and desire to succeed in all of your business objectives. In today's fast-moving world of the internet and social media it is easy to get distracted and spend endless hours lying around and relaxing, but the upside is that there is more useful content available for you now than ever before in the way of books, articles, videos and documentaries, as well as online courses, education and unlimited learning opportunities.

To become successful and earn more money in your

business life you must start to leverage this knowledge to help you grow as a person, which will in turn help you grow your business. The fact that you are reading this book shows that you have the awareness to increase your knowledge and to invest time and energy in yourself.

Self development is not just about knowledge and money. It is about something much bigger than that. It is about becoming the very best you can be in all aspects of your life. The Japanese word "Kaisen" or continual improvement embodies this lifetime goal. In this chapter we will discuss how you can become the ultimate embodiment of success in your life.

We will cover many ideas and methods you can use to help you build a sustainable, successful coaching business. However, they can only be implemented if you have the desire and determination to work hard and develop yourself into a successful coach. I have found through my own personal experiences that the more I have orientated my goals around becoming a better person, a better coach and a better businessman, the more success I have had.

GET FIT

A healthy body certainly leads to a healthy mind: and we are all aware of the many physical and mental benefits that occur when we stay fit. Obviously if we have more energy during the day then we are more productive. But I personally also believe we think smarter, act smarter and get better results in everything we participate in when we exercise regularly.

Keeping fit will improve all aspects of your lifestyle. It reduces stress, frees the mind from worry and builds stamina and self confidence. Take a look at the most successful people in the world – you will see that being fit and healthy is a part of their daily routines. If you hate the fitness centre like I do, then you can find a sport or an activity which you really enjoy doing which doesn't feel like a chore but keeps you fit and energised.

If our body is the machine then what we eat is the petrol – and if what you eat is bad then you will feel bad. Now I am not going to tell you that you have to eat salads for the rest of your life to build a successful coaching business. But if the food you eat is fatty, oily, and doesn't give your body any vitamins, then you will feel lethargic, tired and certainly not motivated to exercise.

I recommend a balanced diet, drinking water, eating some fruit and vegetables, good meats and fish and trying to reduce high sugar fatty foods and alcohol from your diet. A balanced diet will give you energy, help you digest your food correctly and leave you some room for the occasional treat.

MEDITATION & VISUALISATION

This book is not intended to be spiritual, but the powers of meditation and visualisation cannot be underestimated. If we take time to meditate and focus on what we really want from our lives, we are able to achieve some amazing things in a short period of time.

Our brains are congested today, with the unbelievable quantity of messages and thoughts that are thrown at us through television, social media and the internet. Never before have we had so much access to information and opportunities for distraction. If our body is indeed a machine then it is crucial for the maintenance of the machine that we switch it off now and again and let it recover.

Hypnosis and meditation are excellent ways to quieten our minds, relax and reset. Take 15 to 20 minutes out of your hectic life to slow things down and focus. We can completely change our habits, our mindset and our ability to achieve our goals through simple meditation and hypnosis.

Find somewhere quiet and turn all your digital machines to flight mode and focus for four or five minutes solely on your breathing. Relax your body (sit in a chair if you are afraid you will fall asleep). Let thoughts simply pass through your mind without acting upon them or holding on to them. Then begin to visualise your success story, milestones along your journey, happy thoughts and targets you wish to achieve. See yourself becoming the coach you have always dreamt of becoming and all of your goals achieved on a timeline of success.

Doing this exercise on a daily or weekly basis will change your life forever. Not only will you feel more relaxed and in control of your destiny, but you will feel motivated and energised to work hard on your coaching business and achieve your dreams. You will let go of any worries about failure or insecurities about money and success. You will gain confidence in your own abilities and start to recognise more business opportunities when they arise. Success is what we see on the outside, but self development always starts on the inside.

GIVING BACK

Ultimately self development is about finding out who you are as a person and what makes you happy. I know the theme of this book is how to earn more income from your current situation, and we all understand that if we achieve this that our lives will be a little easier. However the wealthiest people in the world all agree that the biggest satisfaction they get out of their wealth is the ability to help others less fortunate then themselves. Yes, we want success, but we need to make sure we are always giving back along the way and helping others improve their situation too. The more you give, the more you will receive in the form of happiness and fulfilment.

PAYING IT FORWARD

Paying it forward is the idea that we do not give in the expectation to get back, but we give free of any expectations and free or any return favours. The only expectation is that the next person also pays it forward and so on and so on.

There are many ways you can give back or pay it forward, and they don't have to be financial. Maybe you can take the time to help somebody else build their business, share your knowledge with young entrepreneurs or give back to other coaches in the way of a book like this one. Just ask yourself "what can I do to help others less fortunate than myself" and see what the immediate ideas are that spring into your mind.

YOUR *FAMOUS FIVE*

It has been said many times that we are the result of the five people we spend most time with. Our opportunities, values and mindset are shaped by what we hear on a daily basis. It is no surprise then that the most successful people on this planet all have like-minded friends and colleagues. Take a look around you and pick out the friends and colleagues who see the world as you do, who are not always complaining about their circumstances or their luck, but are believers in their own development and who look for knowledge in order to improve their happiness and success.

I do not mean for one second you should simply dump all of your friends who do not read or meditate! But if we are heavily influenced by the opinions of those five closest friends or associates then it is imperative that the messages you are hearing are helping you achieve your goals. Try to build a network of motivated, open-minded successful people around you who will push you and encourage you to develop and improve.

Have a look around your club or place of work at the most successful businessmen and women. Can you get some time with them, engage in sport with them, and learn what drives them and what the keys to their success are? Is there a club for self-employed businesspeople that you can join or an online group which you can be part of? Basically, consider anything which will help you increase your opportunities and get you thinking and talking like the successful person you wish to become.

KNOWLEDGE IS STILL POWER

No matter what you hear, you cannot ever have enough knowledge and the wider the spectrum of your knowledge the better you are for it. One of the key things that all successful people have in common is the thirst for knowledge and the continual dedication to educating themselves throughout their lifetimes.

Read or listen to as many books as you possibly can, and watch educational material online or on television. Make it part of your everyday routine and you will start to see a serious upturn in your overall success as a coach and as a businessman or businesswoman. I listen to an audiobook every single time I step into my car or I am travelling somewhere. I used to read books regularly and still have a large bookcase bulging with titles on sport, golf and psychology. However for the last five years I have switched to audiobooks and started to listen to more books on self development, wealth management, success, coaching, sport, fitness, nutrition and well being, as well as history books and fantasy novels. It is absolutely amazing how much knowledge you can acquire in a short period of time and how much of it you can immediately implement into the success of your business.

If you prefer to watch TV or YouTube/Netflix, then be disciplined and watch educational material. It is so easy to waste hours and hours in front of the screen and realise you have not learned anything of any use.

Do not misunderstand me. I also watch YouTube for entertainment sometimes, following my favourite auto channels or sports channels. It helps me relax and switch off, especially after a busy day, and that is also important. But ask yourself each time whether you could be doing something more constructive with my time. Have you finished what you planned to do today, or is this a distraction? If you are honest you will know the answers to those questions.

THE SUCCESS VISION

In my opinion there can be no success in business or in life without a vision. The vision is the blueprint in your mind of where you are going and how you are going to get there. It is the map of success and, like a business without a business plan you cannot achieve anything great without it. I am still on my journey and I have not yet achieved everything I've set out to do. But I have always had a vision in my mind of who I want to become and what I need to do to achieve it.

When I was seven years old living in the southwest of England, I told my mum, apparently out of the blue, that as soon as I was old enough I would be moving abroad. She laughed and asked me why. My answer was "because abroad is where I will make it". I honestly don't know why I said that and how I even came to that outburst but sure enough, at 19 years old, I moved abroad and have never been back to live in the UK.

My vision is closely linked to my passion which is helping others to improve while at the same time improving myself. That is why I became a coach and why I am passionately sharing my knowledge with anyone that will listen to me now. You do not need to be able to predict the future and you do not even need to know yet what your meaning and passion is, but if you are a coach then helping others is at the core of what you do.

You must envision where you want to go and what you want to achieve. This is the roadmap to your success, and without it you will get lost. Take some time to sit quietly and relax your mind, then picture what success looks like for you and what you believe you need to do in order to achieve your goals. The clearer the picture, the easier it is to begin your journey. On tough days when it is difficult to find the motivation to work (and believe me, we all have them) it will be your vision which will motivate you and energise you to keep going and to never give up.

When I began to write this book I was completely overwhelmed by the enormity of the task ahead of me. I knew that I had the knowledge to share and that, when finished, the book could help other coaches become more successful and earn more income. It has been a long tough ride to write this book and on the days where I almost gave up or felt like I couldn't write another word, it was my success vision that motivated me and pushed me to finish the task – and your vision can do the same for you.

A good friend and mentor of mine, Jonathan Wallet, once suggested to me that your success vision should be played backwards in your mind in order to make it achievable. This is a great concept to try out: picture what you want to earn in say two, five or ten years time. Picture how your day looks, how you are working and what hours, picture your lifestyle the cars you are driving, the house you live in and investments you have, picture the wonderful people around you and your holidays and experiences. Picture how you are still learning and helping others and making a difference in your community, and picture the intellectual property you have already created and the successes you have achieved. If you can see it, then you can achieve it.

SUMMARY – CHAPTER ONE

- The very essence of being a coach is continued self development in every area of your life
- Having a healthy lifestyle gives you the necessary energy required to successfully run your coaching business while looking after the important people in your life
- Become as knowledgeable as you possibly can, the more information you have and the wider you read, the more successful you will become
- Visualisation and meditation are excellent ways of programming your mind for success and helping you relax and recharge your body
- Take the time to help other less fortunate than yourself, this can be literally by doing charity work and supporting foundations or by sharing your knowledge to those who need it most
- We are heavily influenced by our environment and the people we spend the most time with. Look at the five people you see most often and ask yourself: Do they motivate you, inspire you and help you become the very best version of yourself?
- Create a success vision or road map to the lifestyle you want to have, this success vision is the energy which will carry you to your objectives and help you overcome obstacles and set backs

MAXIMISING YOUR INCOME

2
THE EVER-CHANGING COACHING LANDSCAPE

Before we go into detail on how to maximise your income now, it is important to look at the current coaching environment and to understand the new challenges that all coaches are facing today. The world of coaching today is unrecognisable compared to coaching back in the late 1980s and 90s. Even in the last 20 years, the environment has undergone tremendous change.

When I started out, a mobile phone could not yet make videos and swing analyses were done with a pen squiggle on footage played back on a TV screen attached to a huge video player. Most coaches were simply good golfers: today's detailed knowledge of nutrition, fitness, biomechanics and ground forces were either unheard of or in their infancy. Now we record a swing on a mobile device, animate it with lines and diagrams, play it in slow motion and record a voiceover, upload it to a coaching platform and send it to our customer within minutes: all from the palm of our hands.

Understanding these giant leaps in technology as well as the knowledge that is available for all to access is one of the keys to developing and operating a modern professional coaching business. Your customers today are not as reliant on your information as they once were: indeed, they are spoilt for choice if they do want to search for new information, a new idea, or a new coach. By understanding the ever-changing coaching environment, you will begin to see how you need to offer unparalleled customer service and value, as well as up to date coaching techniques in order to build strong long-term relationships with your target audience.

TECHNOLOGY ADVANCES

As mentioned above, the use of mobile phones for swing video capture is the norm today, and every sports professional has one. But other technologies have disrupted the coaching landscape and it is important to understand that your current customers know all about them. The likes of Trackman (ballistic ball flight monitors), 3D-analysis software, ground force-plates technology, biomechanics suits and other flight scope technologies have given the golfer and the coach more information about swing dynamics, body geometry, ground pressure and ball flight laws than at any other time in the history of Sport.

As these technologies grow and develop, all coaches will need to understand the basics of them, or be left behind. If you don't have this new knowledge or at least access to the technology, then don't be surprised if potential customers go elsewhere. Do not get me wrong, I do not have all the very latest technologies and I am not suggesting you go out and spend €35`000 on obtaining them right now, but you must regularly attend further education seminars and gain an understanding of the basics in order to share that knowledge with your customers.

THE AVAILABILITY OF INFORMATION

In the developed world, information on just about anything is just a click away, and this means that your customers also have access to literally hundreds of thousands of pieces of information. This wasn't always the case and golfers relied very much on the knowledge of the professional, or on books which they could purchase at the shop (not online). Today a modern coach has to compete with all that information and knowledge, YouTube videos from the top coaches, articles on fitness, strategy, nutrition and the mental aspects of the sport… and that makes our business a lot tougher than it once was.

In order to compete with all that free information, a modern day coach has to develop his or her own content and be a knowledgeable voice to his or her target audience. Any new customer who makes an online search for you needs to be blown away by your profile, the intellectual property you have developed and the qualifications you have, and to realise that you are an expert in your field.

CUSTOMERS DEMAND MORE

Twenty years ago, driving ranges in developed mainland European countries were full, golf was booming and, like tennis before it, golf was a sport in which everybody wanted to get involved and to be part of the new trend. Coaches were hugely in demand and business was easy: agendas were full and there weren't enough hours in the day to serve the demand from customers looking for help. Jump forward 15 years or so and the "Golf boom" has certainly stalled, golf clubs around the world are struggling to find new members and, as of 2020, worldwide golf numbers are receding.

The world of sport is grappling with a new generation, one which has less time and less patience to practise and spend an entire weekend away from home. Clubs and associations are offering more and more flexibility in their membership structures and pricing in order to attract this new generation. However, especially in the world of golf, the days are long gone where a family will pay huge membership fees which tie them to a specific club for years to come.

In golf there are now quicker, shorter playing formats: six- or nine-hole competitions instead of 18 holes and competitions with no prize giving or dinner afterwards in order to accommodate the new audience. Even a relaxation in the famous "dress code" has been introduced all over the world to reduce the barriers to playing golf as well as quicker, more common-sense rules of the game.

The effect on the modern sports coach cannot be underestimated the new audience has less time, less disposable income and more choice and it demands more value than ever before. Also, even with all the advances in technology and knowledge, the average golfer has not improved when measured by their handicap since records were first taken in the 1960s.

Customers are thinking twice about simply spending their money on a lesson, when maybe that money could pay for a quick nine-hole green-fee, or be used for an alternative activity. The end result is that a modern day coach needs to work twice as hard to attract customers, educate them, and improve them (then show them evidence that they have improved) than in the past. I am sure this trend will continue into the future and the days of simply turning up to a full agenda with no questions asked are simply gone: lazy coaches will become a dying breed.

GOLF CLUBS ARE CHANGING THEIR BUSINESS MODELS

As clubs begin to streamline their business models in order to attract a fussier, more dynamic, younger generation of golfers, they too are making it more difficult for a coach to find a place to work as they are no longer willing to pay a retainer (a yearly salary) or support the coach with advertising and marketing.

The effect is that a modern coach must be more flexible than in the past and be prepared to work at multiple venues and facilities. This trend means that clubs and sports centres are becoming more reluctant to employ a full time coach or assist one with their business development. Increasingly, the modern coach is becoming solely responsible for marketing, communication, accounting and business development strategies. If you are to survive these trends then you have to learn the skills necessary to build your own sustainable coaching business.

ASSOCIATIONS & ORGANISATIONS NEED TO MODERNISE

If you are a member of a professional sporting association or organisation you will know that most of them are way behind in educating and preparing modern coaches for the challenges ahead. I know through my personal experience that 95% of the education and material I have seen over the last 20 years has been aimed at making me a better coach and not helping me to understand the fundamentals of building a successful business.

Right now if you want to learn the skills that are required to build a business and stay ahead of the curve then you are more or less forced to educate yourself by reading books such as this one or ones on other subjects like entrepreneurship, business, digital and marketing. Or you need to attend courses and seminars to gather the knowledge needed.

The quicker sporting associations and organisations realise that they need to provide their members with information on the latest technological advances, the latest business ideas and teach their members how to accommodate and improve their service to the ever-changing coaching environment, the better we will all become.

IT IS NOT TOO LATE TO SHINE

The last thing to consider in the current coaching environment is that your competitors also have access to all the knowledge and tools available to you. This means the younger generation of coaches coming through will be very well rehearsed in the ways of social media, online communication tools and digital technology. What the newer generation will lack is the experience and the marketing knowledge needed to produce interesting content and intellectual property.

So this is the time to use your experience and knowledge to build a library of interesting, relevant content which helps your audience improve and gives them tremendous value for their money. If you do this, you will build an audience of customers who trust in you and want to invest in your business ideas. You will be amazed how quickly you can build momentum when you start to implement the strategies in this book, and how positive the reaction will be from your current audience and potential new customers.

SUMMARY – CHAPTER TWO

- Modern technology is changing the way we work and the way we communicate with our customers, we need to understand this trend and adapt our businesses to it.

- There is so much information now available to our customers at a click of a button, and our ideas and techniques will be scrutinised and compared to the top coaches in the world.

- The younger generation of customers are fussier than ever, have less time to dedicate to their chosen sports, and demand a lot more form our products and services. This means we need to adapt our service offerings to meet their needs.

- Businesses and organisations are changing their membership structures in order to meet the demands of the new customer and your coaching business must follow suit in order to stay ahead of the competition.

- Sporting associations and organisations need to adapt their education systems in order to teach coaches how to run a successful modern coaching business.

- It is never too late to learn the skills required to build a successful sustainable coaching business.

MAXIMISING YOUR INCOME

3
CHANGE YOUR BREAD & BUTTER COACHING (EVERYDAY COACHING)

If your main source of income stems from coaching most of the day on a driving range, at a course or in a sports hall, then it is crucial we address immediately how you can both maximise your income on a daily basis and also increase your work enjoyment levels.

Structuring the way you work will have tremendous influence on all the other business opportunities mentioned in this book. You will need to be working efficiently and effectively in order to free up some time and energy for other projects, but without sacrificing any potential income. By working smarter you will begin to see a sudden increase in your income and begin to understand patterns which will lead to even more opportunities.

Simply increasing the price of your services will not be enough to really boost your income, and if you hike the price up too quickly you will even lose customers. Our overall aim is to increase the rate you earn per hour but by setting up systems and practices which increase your income through knock-on sales, commissions and up-sales.

Ideally you have to offer something for everybody within your coaching matrix. Some customers want one-to-one tuition, some demand intensive courses, and others want to participate in group lessons. Take a look at your current services: are you covering the demands and requirements of all your potential audience or are you excluding some potential business?

Below is a little strategy I set for myself many years ago while developing my coaching business. I wanted to make sure I was ticking all the boxes and maximising my potential income in my daily "bread & butter" work (everyday work).

- Offer services which accommodate *ALL* the needs of my customers and potential new customers
- Create the perfect environment to help my customers learn and improve not only their skills but also their overall knowledge and enjoyment of the game

- Increase my hourly rate across the entire spectrum of my services through innovative, creative services

Offer products and services which are associated with the sport, including nutrition & fitness, day trips away, lifestyle products, and well being services

- Move customers from single lessons to group or subscription plans and/or multiple lesson packages
- Offer multiple group lesson activities to increase my hourly rates, as well as helping my customers make new friends and motivate each other to improve
- Offer complete coaching packages that encompass *ALL* the modern technologies and methods available on the market
- Use my ***bread & butter*** coaching as the basis to promote or sell other products & services and funnel customers towards other products
- Sell products and services on top on my daily tuition packages
- Become a key person of influence in the sporting aspects of my customers' lives, by constantly giving them extra value and sharing my knowledge with them

Once I had decided upon this strategy, I set to work preparing new products and services for my target audience. Below we will look at some of the strategies and ideas which can help you build a more exciting, profitable service portfolio.

OVERALL GOAL – MOVE AWAY FROM THE TRADITIONAL ONE HOUR LESSON

As noted in my objectives, it is important that you begin to move away from the traditional "one-hour lesson" business model. This old system of working ten hours a day in the same fashion day after day after day is not only tiring and boring but it also limits how much income you can achieve.

Years ago, if you had a full schedule for the foreseeable future, it was seen as a sign of success, which is possibly the same business model you are following now. However, this system generally leads to coaches losing their motivation through tiredness and the repetitive nature of the work. In the world of golf this is considered one of the reasons why golfers struggle to improve, because keeping students in a training environment and only coaching them technique doesn't improve the skills they require to actually play the game and play it competitively.

If your position is seasonal like mine (in Switzerland) you are pressured to earn as much as possible as quickly as you can: I know I have worked ten hours a day, seven days a week for over seven months in the past to make sure I maximised my income. This meant not seeing my friends, not enjoying the summer months and ending the season completely wrecked and with no motivation to continue.

Let us look now into some ideas for how we can move away from the old structure of working and begin to build a coaching business that is exciting and fun for you, the coach, and that yields higher income and improves the likelihood that your customers are improving and enjoying their tuition.

SUBSCRIPTION PLANS

Many innovative coaches are now starting to move their more motivated customers into subscription plans. The idea of this is that your customer pays a monthly or annual rate for your services instead of paying each lesson on an individual basis. Take the time to sit down with some of your best customers at the end of the season or during the off season, make a season review and then propose this idea to them. When they see that you are motivated to offer them something unique or tailored for their own improvement they will be listening.

THE ADVANTAGES OF THE SUBSCRIPTION PLAN METHOD

Firstly, this idea shows a serious level of commitment from both parties and that this is something that will be well structured and thought out. Within a subscription plan you should be scheduling meetings, practice plans, goal-setting targets and an agreement on how the improvement of the student will be measured over time. Take a holistic approach to your plan and include fitness and nutrition support as well as information on the mental game and strategy. I know many coaches who have offered three different types of subscription plans which cater for different levels of commitment and investment.

The second advantage is that you can begin to structure your training sessions to really meet the needs and requirements of your students without the worry of running out of time or your next student waiting for you in the next room. If your customers are paying on a monthly or yearly basis you can easily structure entire mornings together or more time dedicated to competitive practice or fitness and the mental game.

The third advantage to a subscription plan is the financial one: you will be paid in advance and on a monthly or yearly basis. The general rule of thumb is that customers who pay for subscription plans spend more money on average than if they take individual lessons. If you can build up your participation numbers you will immediately see a boost to your income and experience a new, exciting way in which to work.

PLEASE REMEMBER VALUE

It is crucial that you add extreme value to these plans, meaning that the customer has full use of all your services like a VIP (we will discuss this more later). The idea is that you are going to throw the kitchen sink (everything) at them in order to help them improve their game, and not leave any stone uncovered. You reputation is on the line here, and you need to be able to produce all the material and content you promised in the subscription details. There is no motivation for somebody to sign up to a golf subscription and then receive the same service as all your other customers.

If you do add that extra value then your customers will be telling all their friends about their VIP treatment and all the stops you are pulling out to help them improve. If not, they will be telling anybody who will listen about how you ripped them off!

COMMITMENT INSURANCE

I have typically offered these typed of plans with a commitment clause of a minimum of three months. There is no reason to sign up for a subscription plan if it is not intended for long term improvement, so less than three months really isn't worth it. This agreement shows commitment on both sides and gives you the chance to really show your customers what you can do for them in return for their investment.

After three months, both parties can sit down and discuss the progress of the relationship and iron out any points which are open. Maybe the customer is not practising enough or actually doing any of the tasks you have requested of them? Maybe the customer isn't as committed as he or she originally thought? Or maybe you are not providing the service that the customer expected? The last thing either of you need is another six months working together in an unhappy relationship. This way, after three months and a review you can both decide what is best going forward.

GOLF PACKAGES

Golf packages are a smaller, reduced version of the subscription plan method: they offer unique services and value in a more economical price bracket. It shows a minor commitment from the customer and tells you, the coach, that they are serious about their improvement. Again, you can structure their practice time more efficiently, depending on the content of the package work individually or in a group dynamic.

Tuition packages offer good value to the customer and encourage them to maybe spend a little more than they usually would if they took individual lessons.

I like to add value to my packages and give my customers more than they expected, which often encourages them to sign up to another course or take more lessons in the future. Add a small gift which costs you very little, or include drinks and snacks into the package. Add a bonus lesson or a free article in order to surprise them and show them that you are taking their custom very seriously indeed.

Below is an example of how you can develop a simple package and add value to it, as well as earning a little more than you normally would for the same hours in an individual lesson cycle.

THE ULTIMATE WINTER GOLF PACKAGE

Nov – Apr
4 x 60 minutes individual training

(I've already added an extra hour here as my normal single lessons are 45 minutes)

Nine-Hole Playing Lesson incl. Green-fee and Lunch

(This is a more fun and beneficial working environment and if you try to negotiate a better green-fee rate and a meal deal for lunch it will boost your income)

Fitness Check Up

(Use a professional fitness instructor and negotiate a better price in order to earn a small profit here)

How to Practise at Home Article

(This article will take you up to 30 minutes to write and can be reused over and over again: it is included to simply add value to the package)

Personalised Practice Plan

(Create a template and fill it out for each new customer: again it takes very little time but adds value)

Full access to the XYZ Coaching Platform

(As you are paying a yearly subscription, calculate a small amount for the use of the platform)

10% Discount on all Courses in 20XX

(Offer discounts on other course and packages as a value point for winter package participants: this will also help you funnel customers towards your other services)

You must calculate the **ACTUAL** costs of putting this package together, including the green fee, the fitness check up, your lesson time, the lunch, and the time required for the various plans and administration work. Your customers are not stupid and they will quickly add up in their minds what the true cost of this package could be. If you are able to offer them a price lower than their estimate then it is a winner. Look to get a discount on the fitness check up, the green-fee and the lunch in order to earn a small profit on them. Be prepared to add the practice plan, the article, maybe a small gift, and the discount for your other courses completely for free.

Tuition packages are a great way to boost your income: they offer valuable services to your customers and move away from the old-fashioned "one-hour" business model. Once you have created multiple packages you can reuse them, amend them and improve them over and over again.

A LONG DISTANCE LEARNING OPTION

Much like the subscription plan discussed above, a long distance learning option is a great way to work with anybody anywhere in the world. While on holiday a few years back in

Miami, by pure chance I played nine holes with a gentleman who was interested in improving his golf game. He asked me many questions during the round and wanted my opinion on his game. So naturally I told him where I thought he could make improvements. By the end of the round he asked me if I could coach him long distance Switzerland to Miami.

I flew back to Switzerland and set up a long distance learning course for him making it as professional and efficient as I could. The course offered:

- Use of my online coaching platform whereby he could upload his swing day or night and I would receive a notification and give him feedback on it

- A monthly one-to-one Skype chat to discuss his practice program and his feedback to the swing improvement process

- I constantly added valuable content to his coaching space in the way of practice plan templates, after round review sheets, articles and tips which I had written and links to YouTube media and website which he could benefit from

We agreed on the monthly fee and I inserted the three-month commitment policy, it worked well – even with the time difference we were constantly able to communicate and exchange ideas. "Welcome to the 21st century," I thought, while he was sending me swings from a beautiful sunny Miami and I was reviewing them in freezing cold grey Switzerland.

With today's modern technology we are able to coach anybody anywhere in the world. Use a coaching platform which enables you to upload swings, give voiceover analyses, post links and upload files. You will be surprised how many people want your advice and support, but cannot actually come locally for a "one-to-one" coaching session.

GROUP LESSONS

Integrating more group lessons into your daily business will dramatically increase your hourly rate and your overall income. Setting up small groups of six to eight participants is a highly motivating way to work which offers great value to the customer. Customers enjoy the friendly, fun atmosphere of group training and they will often meet new people and make new friends.

As well as boosting your income through a higher average hourly rate, group lessons give the coach a completely new dynamic coaching environment which is fun to be part of. You can set up workstations and practice games, have your customers playing against each other and give them tasks which they have to complete on their own. If you have multiple groups on any given day, you can use the same theme for each group, meaning that you only need to set it up once and reuse it over and over again.

A good friend of mine has a golf school in Switzerland where one of the coaches runs seven separate groups on a weekly basis which is all paid for in advance at the start of the season: it has become so popular that there is a waiting list for the courses.

The customer sees the group price as providing real value compared to the single lesson price, and I have many customers who only attend my group lessons. Preparation is the key to this way of working: you must know exactly what you want to cover in each session and plan it well in advance. Do not simply turn up at the last minute and try to spontaneously create something or your customers will see straight through it. Prepare hand-outs for the participants and instruction sheets to advise them what they should be doing: this shows them you have planned the session thoughtfully, and it gives them something to take away with them and use again. If you are super-prepared you can even outline what will be covered in each session for the entire duration of the course.

Group lessons are a great way to work and they offer you great opportunities to develop upsales through products and systems which will funnel your customers to the next course you are offering (more on that later). Include coffee breaks or complimentary water to add value: you can also try to get the group to join you for a small after-session drink if possible, to help them bond and make new friendships.

I have personally had huge successes with winter group courses which consisted of six 90-minute sessions, two groups (one in the morning, one in the afternoon) from Nov – Apr, a maximum of eight people per course and summer group courses consisting of 12 sessions throughout the summer months with a maximum of eight participants. Not only was this a great boost to my income but many of the participants signed up for other packages and golf trips on the back of those group activities.

PRACTICE-CLUBS

Practice Clubs are a great option to encourage customers who want to participate in a group atmosphere at a reasonable price. The idea is that you prepare six–eight dates during the season where anybody can simply turn up and learn. These Practice Clubs are between 90 minutes and 120 minutes long and there is no registration needed. The cost is minimal – maybe between €20 & €30 per person per session – and it offers an alternative to private or group lessons.

3 CHANGE YOUR BREAD & BUTTER COACHING (EVERYDAY COACHING)

I have experienced great success with this idea: many customers who had never been to me for lessons before regularly participate in my Practice Clubs. Sometimes I have had up to 15 participants in one session and other times only five, but I have always enjoyed the lesson and over the course of the season earned well above my average hourly rate for them. I personally held the club on a Friday evening and included a drinks session afterwards, which helped the participants bond with one another and created a small tribe of golfers.

The tribe marketing concept is based on the idea of getting small groups together who make friends, start to meet regularly and enjoy activities together. Developing small customer tribes is an excellent way to fill your courses quickly. You will often see these tribes all signing up together to participate in your activities, and as long as you offer them good value and a professional service, they will invest a lot of time and money into you and your business.

You will also be surprised how many of the club members tell their friends about the idea and how suddenly the participation numbers sky rocket. If, on one date nobody turns up, then do some administration work, or some business development, or simply practise.

PRACTICE CLUB
Markgräflerland GC

Adam Lambe

Friday evenings at 18.30 – 20.00
No Registration / Open to Non Members
90 Minutes Group Lesson
Turn up & Practice
5 Dates for 2020
€25 per person
Every week a different theme

PEAK TIME PRICING

In many service industries around the world, peak time pricing is a normal part of business strategy: if demand is high for certain time slots then the price is higher, whereas during quieter periods the price is lower: we are all accustomed to this as part of the demand and supply cycle. In the travel industry, peak time travel costs a premium, and if we want to travel during the holidays or around the festive season we know we have to pay more.

In sport, however, this pricing structure is relatively unusual and the very idea of implementing such a concept makes many coaches shudder. In the future I can guarantee this will be commonplace for all coaches, and it is important that you value your service and your time enough, to begin gradually introducing this concept into your coaching business now.

Look at your schedule and decide which times of the day and week are the most popular: normally this is the weekend slots and the evening slots, as they are the most convenient times for most customers to take lessons. These slots should cost a small premium over the quieter slots, like late morning during the week, which are less frequently booked. This makes absolute economic sense and if a customer wishes to book a lesson in your peak time then they won't be surprised it costs more, just as we know this when we book our holidays.

I have tried to implement this strategy step by step into my business model, by first offering "emergency" lessons which take place either in my lunch break or before or after my official working hours. These emergency time slots are designed to help anyone who immediately needs my time and cannot wait. For this flexibility on my behalf the hourly rate is increased by 50%.

If you are going to work in your lunch break or outside your working hours then you must be compensated for it. This slot will not be filled every week but you will always have customers who desperately want to see you and who will often book at short notice. This is a bonus for you in terms of income and it shows that you are willing to find a solution for your customers when they seek immediate help.

PRICE INCREASE ON SHORT SINGLE LESSONS

Much like the emergency time slot, a shorter quick-fix option in your coaching menu should come with a premium price tag.

In general, you should be aiming to become a coach who wants to develop your customer's improvement over the long term and not offer quick fixes. However, if a quick-fix lesson is requested, say only 30 minutes instead of the normal 60-minute lesson, then again you are well within your rights to charge a small premium for it. If we look at other professions such as doctors, dentists or even therapists, they all charge extra for an emergency session. Now, I am not comparing a golf lesson to emergency medical treatment! Although sometimes it feels like it is the most important thing in the world to my customers, I am simply highlighting the fact that in all other service industries it is commonplace to charge a small premium for an "emergency" session.

I understand that some of our older customers might only be able to physically survive a 30-minute session and therefore they will book them. This is where your experience as a coach comes into play: you can recommend two 30-minute sessions and maybe cover two or three other topics within those 60 minutes, without tiring an older person out.

If your coaching philosophy is based on long-term development then both the emergency lessons and the 30-minute quick-fix sessions can be charged at a premium above the normal lesson structure.

… 3 CHANGE YOUR BREAD & BUTTER COACHING (EVERYDAY COACHING) …

SEMINARS

Seminars are a great way to share your knowledge and skills in a more academic environment and they will help you elevate your reputation as a coach while also earning a increased hourly rate.

The basic seminar structure is to present a theme or topic of interest to an audience using the traditional method of a PowerPoint presentation with a projector and screen or using more modern methods of digital technology such as a telecoms tool or webinar presentation.

Presenting to an audience will help you learn new communication skills as well as showcasing your greater knowledge. Also, the same presentations can be used over and over again for new audiences. The seminar structure actually allows you to communicate to an unlimited amount of new and potential customers depending on the size of the room, if you are doing a traditional presentation, and on how many people have logged in if you are doing an online seminar.

If you have charged your audience a small fee for the seminar then there is no doubt you will be earning a higher hourly rate than giving a single lesson: but make sure you calculate how long the preparation time was and the set up costs and allow for this in the overall price. In order to add value, include a break with drinks and snacks and also allow time for a Q & A session at the end. Record the seminar on video or within your telecoms tool in order to use it for future content and always remember to offer some sort of "next" package, promotion or course at the end.

I have even offered these types of seminars for free and then sold a package or product at the end. One time I just left a bucket at the entrance of the seminar room and asked the participants to pay a voluntary sum depending on what they thought the value of the seminar was to them: this turned out to be a winner.

Invite your own personal customers and give them something different and special, or open it to the entire club and make it a big event, either way your reputation will be enhanced and you will win new customers off the back of it. Some topics I have previously covered in seminars are

The Mental Game of Golf
The 5 Most Important Swing Mistakes Made by Amateurs
Fitness for Golfers
Easy Nutrition for Sport
How Professionals Create Speed
The Modern Golf Swing

3 CHANGE YOUR BREAD & BUTTER COACHING (EVERYDAY COACHING)

HALF DAY/FULL DAY COURSES & WORKSHOPS

Half & Full Day workshops give you the opportunity to showcase your skills over a number of hours in a group coaching environment. Most of the elite coaches from around the world work only in this way, and do not offer anything less than a half day option.

The idea behind this is that the coach is able to spend quality time with the customer and plan multiple activities for their improvement. For the customer it is much more beneficial for their improvement to work like this than it is to simply have a one-hour session with the coach. I recommend this option to most of my elite students, those who are driven to really improve and benefit from my coaching.

This coaching model allows you to really plan and manage exactly what needs to be covered in the course without any time stresses and limitations, and really helps you build stronger relationships with your customers. I have also learnt over the years that many of my customers can plan a half day or full day session with me much better into their busy schedules than a regular single hour or 90-minute session. You can tailor these workshops using themes such as Season Start intensive courses, Summer Camps or "Practise Like A Pro" workshops.

Don't be afraid to mix up the type of tuition you want to present in this format: you can present a small theory session using PowerPoint (a great option when dealing with group workshops) or start the session with a get to know one another planning session. This can be done with a coffee, introduction and some hand-outs to the participants. This type of introduction shows that you are fully professional in your organisation and that you have taken time and effort to prepare, so it will be much appreciated by the participants.

Don't forget to prepare practice sheets, feedback formulas, refreshments and lunch breaks. I even throw in a small participation gift to add value to the course. You need to calculate all these elements in your pricing and (especially with group tuition) you will see a noticeable difference in your income if you start working more regularly in this manner. Any training aids you decide to use within those courses should also be available for your clients to purchase, adding another small bonus to your workshop's income.

GOLF TRIPS, WEEKEND BREAKS & DAYS OUT

Building strong relationships with your customers is a fundamental aspect of a successful coaching business. One of the best ways to do this is to spend time with them outside the normal environment of your coaching facility. Offering trips and days away are a great way to understand your customers on a more personal basis, which will give you important insights into how they tick as human beings and therefore how you can help them learn more effectively.

Some coaches do not like the idea of spending time (or their free time) outside the club with customers. However, not only do you have the potential to earn an income that is much higher than a normal day, but you will also see the future benefits for the other services you offer. When I have taken new customers away on a trip with me they have generally become long-term customers.

Make sure your trips are well organised and well planned: customers really appreciate the time and effort you have put into the trip when they see how well it is running. Giving your customers positive lifelong memories and experiences is one of the most important keys to charging a premium for your services. Always calculate your entire preparation time in the pricing of the trip: this includes organisation, marketing and emailing customers back and forth, not just the time you will be away with them. There is a lot of time and effort that goes into a well planned trip away, and you should be paid for that time.

Always add enormous value to the trip (a common theme throughout this book): give away small prizes or souveniers. They won't cost you a huge amount but they will be well received. If the trip is only a one day away then see if you can get a lunch or dinner included in the overall price and maybe a prize for the best performer of the day.

Most importantly, design these trips exactly how you want them to be, so that you really enjoy the time away and do not see it as a financial must-do evil. Plan the trips around your quieter times where your income is lower, in order to maximise your overall income for the season and communicate with your customers to continually keep them interested in your offers. For instance, where would they like to go next? How could you improve upon the last trip?

FUNNELLING & UPSALES ON ALL ACTIVITIES

One key aspect of boosting income that is often overlooked by coaches is the importance of understanding the concepts of upselling and funnelling. All the courses, seminars, tuition packages and services you offer give you opportunities to sell extra products on top of the income you are already receiving for your time.

3 CHANGE YOUR BREAD & BUTTER COACHING (EVERYDAY COACHING)

Think of which products you can introduce into your coaching business that are beneficial to your customers and will give you an extra income boost. I have implemented this strategy by using training aids within my coaching business and have made them available for purchase at the end of courses or during my sessions. These are training aids which I use and trust anyway, so they are easy for me to support and recommend to my customers.

Another way of implementing these concepts is by offering special discounts during your coaching sessions on other products or other services which you offer. This helps funnel customers from one course to the next and helps you fill future planned courses and packages. These small additions to your daily income can quickly add up and make a substantial difference to a month's income.

All your service offerings should be planned with the relevant products and how you intend to funnel the participants into another one of your courses. I do also know of some coaches who charge a little extra for their services but the products are already included in the price: this of course is another option to consider.

Do not underestimate the importance of this strategy in all of the work you do, these little add-ons are all part of the bigger picture, helping you maximise your coaching income. Now we will look in more detail at what type of products you could consider and how you can build other new streams of income into your business strategy.

SUMMARY – CHAPTER THREE

- Create products and services which maximise your income while helping you move away from the traditional "one hour" lesson structure
- Structure your working weeks in a way that will help you enjoy your job, offer high quality services and are economically viable
- Offer products and services which meet **ALL** the demands and needs of your customers
- Make it your business goal to upgrade your customers from single lessons and package to long term improvement plans and subscriptions
- Group lessons and activities offer your customers a different learning experience and better value for money, while increasing your own hourly rate of income
- Consider peak time pricing and emergency lessons to boost your income when demand for your services are high
- Organise seminars and workshops to help you showcase your knowledge and your academic abilities while offering your customers alternative ways in which they can learn.
- Never forget the **Up-sales!** Selling products at the end of your courses and workshops is a great way to boost your income while offering a professional service to your customers

4
PRODUCT SALES & SERVICE COMMISSIONS – THE NEXT GEAR TO HIGHER EARNINGS

The first steps to maximising your income and improving your coaching business are changing your coaching model or "bread & butter" to offer smarter services, increasing your appeal to potential new customers and increasing your hourly rate.

The next step is to open your mind to possible new streams of income and begin the journey to even higher earnings. As we have discussed, coaches are always fighting the age-old enemy of time: even if you work 24/7, boost your income with product upsales and funnel your customers to new services, you are still limited in how much you can actually earn. I want to remove that ceiling for you and your coaching business, and open the door to unlimited opportunities to maximise your income: you are only restricted by your imagination.

In this chapter we will look at some of the products and services which you could offer to add to your already increasing income.

PRODUCTS — IN DETAIL

As mentioned in the last chapter, one of the quickest and easiest ways to boost your overall income is to introduce products as part of your service offering. Any product which you truly believe in and maybe even use yourself is something of value to your customers.

When deciding which products you wish to sell try to remember that your intention is to help your customers and add value to their experience, not simply to earn a quick buck or two. Too many coaches sell products which have high margins but are of little use to their customers. Never forget that if you try and sell useless or poor quality goods to your customers, your reputation will be tarnished.

BUY IN BULK

Once you have decided to sell certain products then it is important to be able to buy them at a trade price: this normally means buying in bulk. Having more of a product in stock will also motivate you to sell them and remind you to introduce them into your sales strategies. Find a source from which you can purchase your products, and negotiate the best possible price you can. If you know that you are able to sell hundreds of a particular product then you will be able to get an even better deal. Never stock products in mass if you are not sure that you can sell them, as that is income wasted. Instead, take the time to consider exactly what you wish to sell and in which scenarios you can promote them.

FIND A VALUABLE SOURCE

If you are unable to stock the products yourself then find a person or a company you can source them from. Again you must have a better price than a normal customer and the products must be available when you need them: nobody likes to be promised something and then still be waiting for it weeks later. If you cannot get a better price then negotiate a commission for every product you sell, this way, it is beneficial to both parties.

If you have products on hand and you can show them to your customers or even let them try them out, there is no problem with them ordering one and having it delivered to their house or picked up directly from you. Do not recommend products to customers and then tell them to order by themselves, this is not the service they will expect and it is likely you will lose out on sales.

INCLUDE YOUR PRODUCTS IN YOUR COACHING

Make sure your products are always available, always seen and always used within your training sessions: if you do this, your customers will consistently ask you about them and wonder where they can buy them from.

DON'T RESTRICT YOUR PRODUCTS TO YOUR SPORT

Products such as training aids, fitness aids, clothing or general lifestyle and wellness products all have a place within your coaching business. My customers constantly ask me what they should buy and what I would recommend for them. Do not be afraid to recommend and sell products which help your customers in any other part of their life.

I know of a coach who successfully sells mattresses as a part of his coaching business. He wants his customers to have a better night's sleep in order to help them feel more energised and motivated, and they are thankful for it. In the sporting field, we can incorporate many different industries into our sales portfolio: as long as it is beneficial to our customers and you can truly stand behind the products, then anything is possible.

PROMOTION & ADVERTISING

Once you have decided which products you want to sell, think in detail about how you will promote these products. I have found that most companies are willing to send you some sort of promotional material to help you display products or simply to inform customers of the product benefits and advantage.

If you cannot get hold of that information then search the internet and look for quotes and content showing your products in action and the positive feedback previous customers have given. Worst case scenario is that you have to produce your own marketing material in the way of a PDF, flier or a slide show/PowerPoint presentation. It is always good to have something to hand out to interested parties.

DESIGN YOUR OWN PRODUCTS

We will talk more later in this book about creating rather than consuming as a business philosophy: at this point I would just say you shouldn't disregard the idea of actually developing and building your own line of products. If you have a good idea for a new product or believe you can improve upon a current product then look into how you can create your own brand.

This is a lot easier than you may think: the world has become a very small place with the internet, and a quick email or message to a manufacturing plant in Asia or Northern America will link you very quickly to somebody who can make your vision a reality. Websites such as Alibaba also open the door to thousands of production centres and manufacturers who will produce just about anything for you at a very fair price.

I built a small online shop and had all my products produced in Asia or in the USA: they are made with my own personal branding and packaging. It was a process that was a lot easier than I could have ever believed. Sometimes investing in your own products is much more beneficial to your income than buying other companies' products and sharing the commission and profits with them.

BUILD RECOMMENDATION LISTS

One good way to introduce your products to your customers is by creating regular product recommendation lists. This can be found on your website or on an online shop (more on that later) and included weekly or monthly in your newsletter. If your customers have a detailed review of the products you are offering them and understand the benefits and value of them, then they will be encouraged to purchase them from you.

Many years ago I found I was constantly being asked by my customers which books they should buy and read, so I decided to open an affiliate marketing account with Amazon and to begin to build a monthly recommended reading list. Each month I would select a relevant title, one which I had read and enjoyed, and I would write a small review about the book for my customers. Then I set up a page on my website where one could purchase the book directly. I advertised the list in my regular newsletters and on my webpage, and reviewed a new book every month: and guess what? Yes, I began to sell an increasing number of books through that link, making a small commission on each one.

Later we will go into more detail about online sales and how to earn extra income via social media and the internet but it goes without saying that product reviews via YouTube or Vimeo are a great way to promote products and win sales.

BECOME A DISTRIBUTOR

If you wish to take selling products to another level, then consider becoming a distributor yourself. If you find a product, which you truly believe in and you see the potential to generate income selling it, then contact the manufacturer and see if you can take the distribution licence for your area or country.

Now of course you could argue "but I won't have time for that, because I am coaching 100%!" But actually if you work smarter you will be working less and earning more, and therefore you will have more time for business development.

Investigate a product and see if you can sell through multiple channels such as the internet or B2C. If you have no way of personally investing the time to meet potential customers, then employ someone who is paid on a commission basis.

Maybe somebody you already know is on the road selling other products and they will happily promote yours too; or maybe it is somebody who wants to build up the business for you while receiving good commission on the sales.

In the modern world of digital and automation you can more or less decide how involved you want to be in the entire sales process. Usually the more you have to do, the more you can earn. But some manufacturers are happy for you to do the promotion, advertising and lead generation and they will simply ship the product directly to the customer, a system known as drop shipping.

Be aware that there are often licence fees and minimum purchase requirements associated with distribution rights, and make sure you have calculated all the costs and risks before diving in and signing the contract. Also develop a clear cut strategy for exactly how you will promote the product and to whom. You should never take on a distribution licence which requires hefty initial investments of both time and money.

AFFILIATE MARKETING PRODUCT SALES

If the distribution idea sounds a little overwhelming then do not fear: there are plenty of manufacturers out there offering affiliate marketing solutions. An affiliate program is quite simple: you have a contract with a company to promote and sell their products, you create leads (potential customers) and for every sale you make, you receive a commission.

This can be set up through a sales page on a website or through email marketing and word of mouth. Much of the current sales revenues associated with social media and video platforms are structured in this way, with affiliate marketers promoting products and influencers being paid to use certain brands within their story boards.

Affiliate marketing takes much of the stress away from selling products, as you are not required to pre-purchase stock or pay any license fees. Most affiliate systems are automated: a potential customer simply clicks through a link you have developed and, if they purchase the product, you win. The negative side of this system is that the commission is much smaller than the normal profit margins of becoming a wholesaler or distributor (unless the product is very expensive) as you play a much smaller role in the entire process.

GENERAL COMMISSIONS

You don't only have to sell products to earn money. There are other ways you can get commissions or discounts for your lead generation. Look to set up partnerships with local companies in your area who are prepared to pay you a small commission if you bring them new customers.

Think of businesses your customers may already visit or would visit if there was a discount or deal in it for them. Businesses such as hairdresser's beauty salons and spas, restaurants and fitness centres or a popular wine shop in your area, these are the types of businesses that can really profit from new customers and you can help them.

Organise a small discount for your customers if they frequent that shop or facility for the first time (maybe design a small business card-sized discount voucher and hand them to your customers) and when they turn up with their card you receive a small bonus or a personal discount for yourself which saves you money too.

We will discuss partnerships in more detail later, but if you have multiple business agreements in place with local companies you will be surprised by how quickly your income can grow and how many new opportunities will open up for you.

REDUCTIONS FOR YOU

If a commission-based agreement is not an option for you, then look for discounts if you recommend new customers: saving money on your own products and services is just as vital as earning more money. Will the local top restaurant give you a discount or a free bottle of wine on the house next time you visit? Will the fitness centre discount your membership because you sent them four new customers last year?

Any time you save money you are increasing your purchasing power and your overall usable income, and this contributes to your overall wealth and ability to venture into new businesses and buy new products. If your customers were going to join that fitness centre anyway or dine in that local restaurant, why should you not be able to profit from it and offer your customers better value?

WRITE ARTICLES AND A BOOK

Writing articles which can be published or sold to a magazine is another way you can develop a product to sell. If you have enough content, consider writing a book like this one and having it published or made available online as an eBook or audiobook. Products do not necessarily need to be physical, and if you are as passionate about sharing your knowledge as me, then do not underestimate what you are capable of producing.

This could start with a simple blog or a part of on your newsletter each month where you write your thoughts down on trending topics. If you get good feedback and want to monetise this idea send a copy of your work to a local or national magazine or trade journal and see if they are willing to publish your articles. If they like your work and your style they may ask for a series of articles.

I am a passionate writer and also passionate about sharing my knowledge with others. I have written blogs for years, and this book is more or less a collection of the ideas and knowledge I have accumulated over the last 20 years. Never start out with the single goal of writing to earn money or you may be quickly disappointed: always use your intellectual property as part of your overall service offering, albeit one that will certainly open new doors for you.

The costs associated with publishing a book have dropped tremendously over the last ten years or so and it has never been easier to market, sell and distribute your work. As well as the opportunity to increase your income with a book, you will also boost your reputation as a coach and also open up more academic opportunities for you, such as presentations, webinars and speeches. Maybe you will love it so much that you write an entire series of books?

Next, let's look at some other things to consider when maximising your income...

RENT OR SELL OLD EQUIPMENT

If you are anything like me then you have a ton of old, used or even new equipment which you ordered for yourself and no longer use. You can obviously sell this equipment on sites such as eBay, Facebook Marketplace or any other free online market platforms. Another idea would be to rent out your old equipment to visitors or even to your facility for a small charge. Maybe you received the equipment at a discounted or wholesale price and therefore you can make a reasonable profit from it. If you are never going to use it, then get rid of it and invest the profit into some other part of your business.

For years I collected rare and expensive putters and had a lovely bag in my spare room with around 15 putters in it. One day I realised that I couldn't care less about the putters anymore and that it was just dead money sitting there, so I went about selling each and every one of them. Unbelievably, I ended up with around €4000 in my bank account by the time the last one sold: some of them were genuinely rare and expensive although I sold most of them for around €240. Have a look in your garage or spare room and see what equipment you have collected over the years: do you really need it? If not, can you rent it or sell it and invest the money somewhere else? [1]

EQUIPMENT REPAIR AND RENOVATION

In our PGA apprenticeship we learnt how to build and repair golf equipment: this is the kind of skill you can monetise to boost your income. If you are qualified to repair and even renovate equipment then offer this service as part of your coaching business. Buy in the tools you need and make a space at your facility or club, or even in your cellar or garage, and begin working.

---

[1] Please do not sell brand new "own use" discounted equipment which you received at trade price for a full price unless you are an official account holder of that manufacturer. It is poor professional conduct to order equipment on own personal use terms with the intention to sell it on at a new price.

MAXIMISING YOUR INCOME

If your local facility does not offer this type of service, then make sure you offer it for them: as golf professionals this could involve grip changes, fitting new shafts and club heads or even fitting customers for new equipment, all of which you can charge a competitive rate for.

I have a good friend who offers this type of service. During the off season he can earn up to €400 a week repairing clubs and changing grips, in a time period when he has less income and more spare time. He also offers these services during the peak season and does the repairs at weekends or on his days off, which simply boosts his overall monthly income.

If you wish to take this idea to another level then consider becoming a specialist "fitter" who stocks branded equipment and custom-fits tailor-made sets. If you can get the license to a well known manufacturer, and customers seeking this brand are recommended to you, then you can earn double income on the process, firstly from the fitting process and secondly from commission on equipment sales.

As you look outside of your current nine-to-five environment you will begin to see many opportunities to increase your income and open new doors. The examples above can be adapted for any sports coaching business and can serve to spark your imagination into action. Have a think about how you can explore some of the opportunities outlined in this chapter and begin to develop new streams of income.

SUMMARY – CHAPTER FOUR

- Source useful products at good prices and make them available for your customers, do not restrict the products to your industry, anything that can help your customers improve, feel better about themselves or help their lifestyle is valuable

- Before investing money in products develop a strategy on exactly how you will sell them and to whom

- Design recommendation lists which show the benefits of your products and include them in all communications to your customers

- If you wish to increase your income and start to build your own brand then considering designing and producing your own products

- If you wish to earn commissions on products but do not have the income, time or knowledge to source them, then look at distribution opportunities and affiliate marketing options

- If you don't want to invest in tangible products, then consider selling educational material such as online courses, eBooks and articles

- Reductions and discounts for you in return for introducing customers to local businesses are just as valuable as commissions and revenue. See if you can build relationships with businesses such as hairdressers, fitness centres and restaurants

MAXIMISING YOUR INCOME

5
CUSTOMER ACQUISITION & RETENTION

A successful modern sports coaching business, needs to place customer acquisition, customer growth and customer retention at the centre of its business strategy. We have looked at some customer growth strategies already within the first few chapters by changing the way we work on a daily basis and how we can offer more valuable products and services, we will examine more methods later on. This chapter focuses on where we can find new customers and how we will retain our current ones.

The top coaches are excellent at building their customer base year on year and producing engaging content as well as interesting courses for their audiences. This strategy is almost guaranteed to make your coaching business a success, and, with more and more new customers on tap to purchase your products and services, you will be well on your way to higher earnings.

You objective must be to build strong relationships with your current audience and develop new, innovative ideas to win new customers. This will be achieved by communicating well with your overall target audience, and measured by how well you are received by them and what kind of activities and courses you offer. If potential customers see you developing exciting products and services as well as offering good value they will support and follow you.

In this chapter we look in depth at some of the ways you can immediately start to build your personal customer base and then look at which communication tools you will need to keep them engaged and happy.

CUSTOMER ACQUISITION IN GENERAL

The first place to look when building your customer base up is in your own club or working facility. This is where most of your current customers spend their leisure time and where potential new customers can most easily be won.

Let us look at some of the activities and strategies you can adopt in order to build up your own customer base and drive your coaching business forwards.

5 CUSTOMER ACQUISITION & RETENTION

HANG UP INFORMATION

Now this may seem obvious but never underestimate the importance of having information about yourself and your services hung up in areas where every member and visitor can clearly see it. This shows your audience that you are active and looking to help them with their improvement. Hang up useful tips and warm up instructions, which every member can use. Even better a small card to take away which illustrates five important keys for consistency or the common mistakes most amateurs make.

If you want to take this idea into the 21st century have a QR code hanging on the wall (or on your business card) which sends users directly to a website page which has all your tips and information on it. Regardless of how you choose to do it, make sure everybody can see who you are, what you offer and provide something of value to them which will encourage them to dig a little deeper into you and your services.

All contact information, price lists, seminars, courses and activities must be available for everybody to see. If there isn't currently a spot for you, then get onto the manager and ask where you can advertise your business: maybe you have to buy a small display case and screw it to the wall yourself or set up a small table in the entrance with your card and a business flier on it.

TRADITIONAL FLYER OR BROCHURE

We will go into detail on some of the more modern approaches to running a successful coaching business in this book, but do not think for a second that all of the old-fashioned methods are dead.

Producing a simple flyer or brochure is a fantastically effective way of promoting you and your business. It does not need to be anything fancy or printed on expensive paper nor does it need to be designed by an exclusive marketing house: it can be something that you designed at home using a relatively inexpensive program and printed by an online company for an economical price.

Flyers and brochures are ideal for interested customers to simply pick up and take home with them so they can browse through your coaching products and services in their own time. Be sure to include all your important contact information and your website details, and I can recommend you include some sort of "new customer" discount or promotion which is aimed exactly at that target audience.

EMAIL SUBSCRIBER LIST

Building up your email contact list should be one of your main business objectives, as it gives you a wider range of future business opportunities and potential feedback. Hanging up a simple email subscriber list on a notice board or close to your working area is a great way to pick up new customers with very little effort.

You can create a teaser article or a tips & advice page next to the list, which will be sent to any new subscriber. This way, there is automatically value for anybody who signs up. Adding one or two new customers every month to your list can really make a difference to your participation numbers and your overall customer exposure.

OTHER SERVICES

We mentioned in the previous chapter that services such as club repairs or custom-fitting equipment can help you boost your income, but let us not forget that these services will also put you in contact with potential new customers.

I have often acquired new customers through a club fitting procedure, because I have helped them to improve one or two technical things in order for them to profit more from the new equipment. These kinds of services, alongside your tuition packages, open the door to completely new customers who were not initially coming to you for a lesson, but who end up leaving thinking how professional and knowledgeable you are, which bodes well for your reputation and future custom. What services can you offer your members or your club that will put you in contact with new members and, potentially, new customers?

THE CLUB LIFE

One of the quickest and most effective ways to meet new people and reach out to new customers is by involving yourself in the community of your club or facility. Begin to help out at competitions or events as a starter or you could do the prize giving. Be on hand to talk to the members so they can get to know you and understand who you are as a character and what knowledge you possess. Even better would be to organise your own event for the members or co-sponsor an existing event. However you decide to help out you must be seen and involved in the life of the club: this kind of engagement is worth its weight in gold in terms of winning new customers.

I have heard many coaches telling me that they do their work and leave the club as quickly as they possibly can. This is an old-fashioned way of thinking: the modern sports coach is an intricate part of the club life and shares the passion and love of the sport with its members.

When I first started at my current golf club I knew nobody, so every day I would walk along the driving range and introduce myself to the members. Then I started to play in the club competitions just for fun on my days off, and I helped out at some of the events and did a few prize giving's. Finally I wrote a letter to the members introducing myself and sharing my philosophy on coaching and a little information on my background and upbringing. Within months, everybody in the club knew who I was and business started to build.

5 CUSTOMER ACQUISITION & RETENTION

Only last year I was told by an older member of the club how wonderful it is to see me at weekends playing on the course and spending time around the clubhouse. Now I also have a wife and family and cannot be 24/7 at the club, but popping in for a few hours or joining a monthly competition goes a long way towards making a positive impression on the members. Unfortunately, the coaches that are seen running for their cars the very second they have finished their last lesson leave a very different impression on the members.

ORGANISE EVENTS FOR NEWCOMERS AND BEGINNERS

A steady stream of beginners and newcomers is the future lifeline of any club or association, and as a coach we play a major role in the development and education of a beginner. How we educate and interact with them, will often determine whether or not they stay in the sport.

It is important to organise introductory courses and open days for newcomers to try your sport out in a friendly, non-judgemental environment. If your club or facility already organises this then you need to be a big part of it, as you have the skills to leave the best impression on people. If this is not that case at your facility, then you need to be the one who initiates these programs. Often somebody who starts the sport with you will become a lifetime customer and I do not need to explain how that can affect your income. Seek the support of your club and organise an open day or an introductory course for the public and take the lead role in the event.

Another good member's event which is popular today is a "bring a friend" day. This is where current club members invite their non-playing friends to enjoy their passion for the day. These events are always well received as the non-playing guests get to see exactly what all the fuss is about and get to try out the sport. Try to organise a lunch or a dinner to accompany this event and it will make a great day out for everyone. If you can be paid a small amount for your time in these events, then great, but don't worry if not because, if one of the newcomers decides they love the new sport and they want to begin immediately, who will they be contacting...?

BE INNOVATIVE & CREATIVE

When you get down to planning your next season's courses, consider offering something a little more innovative and creative, rather than only sticking to the same template over and over again. Most coaches seem to offer the same old courses and there really isn't anything to separate them

Think how you can do it differently and stand out from the other coaches by offering special courses for certain demographics like, for example, a "singles club" or a course which is organised only for "business men and women". What about a mum & daughter or a dad & son course? The courses should be set up to accommodate the time of the day the specific demographic is available and be advertised accordingly.

I have set up "practice clubs" on a Friday evening which are a simple turn up and practice affair, with no registration needed and a minimal cost. I advertised these courses as something to which you can "turn up and practice, meet new people and learn new skills". This was the perfect course for some of the members who generally play alone or don't know many people within the club. We always sit down together and have a drink together and my participants make new friends.

Think a little outside the box and offer something nobody else is doing. Look at the demographics of your club and decide what is feasible and what would be well received. Then look outside of your club at local businesses and see if you can encourage them to come to a lunch break sports session for body and mind, as a stress reliever for the everyday office workload. There are opportunities for new streams of income everywhere if you can be a little creative and brave enough to test them out.

LOOK TO THE MEMBERS' SECTIONS WITHIN YOUR CLUB

In any active club there are groups of members who organise their own events and play regularly together. This is certainly the case in tennis and golf clubs. The sections are normally split into juniors, seniors, ladies and men's and they are the heartbeat of the club. Quite often the club teams who play in local and national leagues are made up of players from these different sections.

When developing a strategy for building up your personal customer base these club sections are your absolute bread and butter. The sections are made up of the most passionate, motivated members of the club, who are already investing huge amounts of time and money in their chosen sport.

To improve as a coach it is important that you work with all levels of students and push your coaching skills to the limit. Team and Section Group coaching is one way to help you develop your coaching skills, as well as increasing your hourly income. The dynamics are very different and the expectations are too: but by involving yourself in the development of the different sections you can greatly increase your reputation and place yourself in the very heart of club life.

Contact each captain or section leader and explain what it is you can do to help their section improve. Maybe even consider offering a "Free" introductory course first and then a series of group lessons throughout the season. Do not try and charge the club sections an exorbitant rate for coaching: the likelihood is that you will gain some private students from the sections anyway and your aim should be to build a long-term relationship with them.

Too often I hear about greedy coaches who are not willing to make any deals or offers for members' sections and end up losing out in the long term.

SOUND BOARDING AND FEEDBACK

One great method of improving the relationships you have with your current customers is by involving them in your product and service development process. Use a group of your most loyal customers for sound boarding new ideas and getting feedback about courses, trips and products you are considering.

You will receive open and honest feedback on your ideas from this group, and establish if the pricing is fair or not. When you do then develop that idea with their involvement they will feel an emotional attachment to it and will probably support it financially.

Sound boarding is a professional method of business development and an excellent way to build interest and excitement into your product and service development. Many manufacturers use this method before releasing a new product in order to build hype and pre-sales before its release date.

VALUE IS THE RETENTION KEY

If you have followed the ideas and methods outlined in this chapter, then you are well on your way to building a strong customer base. The next step in that process is retaining those new customers, which becomes harder and harder to do as your coaching business grows and your availability decreases.

The most obvious way to keep your entire customer base engaged is through your content and media. This means consistently producing useful, beneficial content for your customers to enjoy. This can be done through articles, videos or webinars and through useful information links and websites advertised in your newsletter. If every message they receive is a sales pitch they will soon begin to question the value they are getting by supporting you and your business.

The smallest things can also make a difference, like staying in touch with customers you have not seen in a few weeks: a quick message or telephone call asking them how they are and how is their game; walking through the middle of the restaurant and acknowledging and greeting you customers rather than avoiding them; and taking a few seconds more to listen to them when they begin to explain their problems. These are all ways to stay connected to your customers.

Other ways you can improve your retention rates are by offering discounts for certain products; organising thank you parties; or giving your customers a small gift or thank you letter just to know them that you appreciate their business. Setting up some sort of customer loyalty program is another way of giving something back to your customers and saying thank you.

I have personally held an end of season get together with my customers where the drinks and snacks were on me and I set up an indoor golf course with fun games and prizes. This has cost me up to €500 in the past but it has always been very well received and I have really enjoyed the opportunity to show my customers that I appreciate their support and that I take nothing for granted.

SUMMARY – CHAPTER FIVE

- Always look firstly within your own working environment when developing a customer acquisition strategy
- The traditional methods of advertising are just as important today as they were 15 years ago. Designing flyers and brochures and hanging important information up on notice boards will still help you grow your coaching business
- Collect email addresses in order to build your customer base, and send regular newsletters with your products and services
- Create innovative and interesting events in which you give yourself the opportunity to meet potential customers
- Use your current customer base to sound board new ideas and allow them to be involved in your services, this will motivate them to help you make your ideas a success and give your some truthful feedback
- Customer acquisition is important to help your business grow, but retaining your current customers is the most important of all and the key to that is adding value to everything you do

6
MUST-HAVE COMMUNICATION TOOLS

Now that we have covered some methods for building your customer base offline, it is time to switch our attention to the huge potential of the online environment. Getting exposure has never been easier than it is today and there are so many channels via which you can promote your coaching philosophy and build up a dedicated following.

We will look at how you can maximise your income using modern digital channels in another chapter but our focus here is still on building and retaining our customer base. Each technology which I recommend in this chapter can be used for both customer acquisition and as a communication tool.

The key thing to remember is that the world of digital technology is actually a simple, quick way to spread your message, your brand and your services. Think of it as a supersonic microphone which can immediately speak to the world. Your aim as the coach is to use this microphone and talk to the masses in order to get your message across to them. Once you have begun to build a strong customer base, it is vital to continually share valuable information with them and keep reinforcing their belief that you are the right coach for them.

YOUR WEBSITE
Customer Acquisition

The first step any potential customer is going to take when looking for a new coach is likely to be an online search. This search may contain key words such as Tennis Coach near me, or Golf Professional in the region xyz. If you do not have an online presence (or only a Facebook page) nobody is going to find you in their search. They will, however, find the details for all the other local coaches who do have an online presence and an appealing website.

In the modern technological world we live in today, web searches are used for almost everything, even looking for a house, holiday or a new camera. So, if you are not at that party you will lose out on potential business. For a serious coaching business I believe it is an absolute "must" to have a website and be findable in a web search. This website could be a simple business card layout with all your important information and contact details on it, or it could be a multi-dimensional website with tons and tons of interesting content available. Either way you must at least have something.

Think of a website as one of the all important touch points for somebody who has never met you and knows nothing about you and you're coaching. What kind of impression will it leave? Will a potential customer be encouraged to reach out to you after seeing your website? Is it clear who you are and what you offer? By answering these questions you can build a simple but effective website.

As a Communication Tool

As a communication tool, a website can house all your important information and be the hub of all your promotional activity. This means all the communications you send out via social media or in your newsletter can lead your customers back to a page on your website via a clickable link. My personal method is that the website contains all my articles, downloads, contact and course information. All my customers know they can find everything they need on my website. My website address is on my business card as well as in the signature of my emails.

It is crucial for you to keep your website updated and to continually add and improve the information on it. There is nothing worse for your reputation then to see that the last update or last activity on your website was over six months ago: your customers will think you have stopped working or that you are no longer prepared to add value to your services.

You can use your website to showcase all your skills, your other social media channels, your products and a newsletter sign-up option for those who have not yet registered. Make sure your website is secure with a registered SSL key (especially if you want to sell products on it) and that you communicate to your users exactly how you will be handling their data. Build the website with search engine optimised (SEO) key words and produce interesting relevant content in order to help the search engines rate your site. Any professional web designer will point you in the right direction, and there are various companies who offer build-your-own-website services.

NEWSLETTER/EMAIL MARKETING
Customer Acquisition

A newsletter is an excellent way to introduce you and your services to a potential new customer. The only stepping stone is that you need their email address and their consent to add them to your list. This is why the offline activities mentioned in the last chapter are so important. Make sure you give potential new customers ample opportunities to sign up to your mailing list: this can be after introduction courses, after open days, or through a list hanging next to your information on a notice board in your club.

I have had a lot of success from handing out a newsletter sign-up list to different sections of my club after they have had a small seminar or competition with me. Once they have signed up it is my responsibility to convince them that I can help with their improvement, through my communications, free content and articles. There are a number of customers on my mailing list who read my blogs, watch my videos and enjoy my content but have never actually been on a course or taken a lesson with me. This is fine. I just haven't quite persuaded them yet that I am the right coach for them: and at some point I will find a way to offer exactly the right service for them.

As a Communication Tool

As a communication tool, email marketing and the use of a newsletter is probably quite obvious to you, but I am constantly amazed by how few sports professionals and coaches use this tool with their customers. A regular email message or newsletter is a must for a modern coaching business and there are many email providers who, for a small monthly fee, can offer you an excellent platform full of professional templates and analytics tools.

If you link your email provider account with your website you can have any new customers who sign up to your newsletter directly integrated into your lists, helping you automate the email customer base list. One of the great advantages of this is that it enables you to build different types of customer lists and segment different demographics within your audience. You can then choose which mails go to which customers. This becomes crucial when you start to use the insights and analytics services provided by your email platform. They will show you how many people opened your mail, how many recipients clicked on a link and give general feedback on how highly your content is rated. (See picture below)

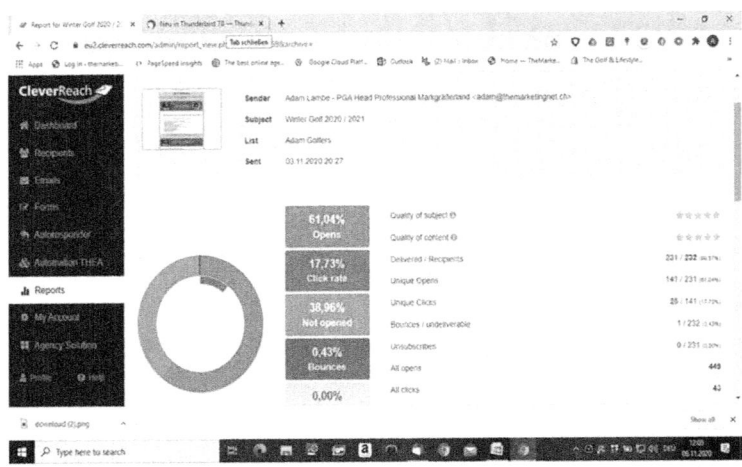

THIS IS A TYPICAL ANALYTICS PAGE OF AN EMAIL PROVIDER

So, once you have designed your template (or many templates) you can easily amend them each month and add new information including new links to pages on your website or links to social media content and videos. This type of communication is very much a targeted strategy, as you know exactly who has received, opened, read and acted upon your messages. This helps you to see what type of content is working well and what you need to change in order to get more audience engagement.

If your open rates are high and your customers are clicking through to your website then the content is good. There is strong evidence to suggest that the average person needs to see the same promotion up to five times before they react to it. Now we certainly do not want to spam our customers with the same message over and over again, so design your newsletter carefully, keeping some of the promotions but changing others.

A good guide is to use the 80-20 percentage marketing strategy: 80% useful, relevant information (providing value for your customers) and 20% promotional sales content.

Try to send out a regular email or newsletter at the same time every week or every two weeks: then your customers will be in a rhythm of receiving your latest information. Plan your newsletter in advance and consider how useful the information is going to be – do not get in the habit of simply adding content for contents sake.

SOCIAL MEDIA
Customer Acquisition

Social media today is a highly important part of your communication strategy: it allows you to share your message with the entire world, attract new customers and to start building a personal brand. Each social media platform has a different demographic and not all platforms are useful in regards to acquiring new customers. My customer base is generally between 40 and 65 years old, so advertising my products and services on platforms such as TikTok is not going to win me any new customers, unless my specific strategy is to attract a younger fan base.

Look at the demographics of your current customer base: what age are they? Then begin to devise a strategy based on what social media channels they are likely to use. If this age group is your intended target audience then you need to start producing content aimed at that demographic and to use the corresponding social media channel.

I produce content primarily for Facebook, YouTube & LinkedIn. This fits my ideal customer demographic: middle aged professionals who are passionate about their golf games as well as having the financial means to invest in their personal development.

Social media channels are an excellent way of sharing your information and showcasing your skills to the entire world, and at no financial cost. They are simple to use and will speak immediately to hundreds of potential customers. So try to imagine who your "perfect" customer is and produce content which is aimed directly at them.

If you have an upcoming course or new product you really want to push, then you always have the option of paying for social media advertising which boosts how many people will see your posts. This is a great way of attracting potential customers and appealing to a wider audience: and it is a relatively inexpensive method compared to the amount of exposure it gives you.

As a Communication Tool

As a communication tool, Social Media is an integral part of communication strategy: I share all my latest news and content consistently across my channels. Some of my content is specifically for one channel in terms of its message, while other content is produced for all channels. As I run multiple businesses and promote many products, it is a fine line between spamming my audience with sales information and still giving them value for their support. As I mentioned, following the 80-20 rule (80% valuable content & 20% sales) is a great way of adding value for your audience as well as promoting your products and services.

A good strategy to adopt for social media communication is to promote all of your content with web links that direct users back to your personal website. This gets potential customers visiting your website, where they might uncover more great content which will encourage them to either look further into your services or even sign up to your newsletter.

If you create and share different formats of content like videos, blogs, articles and podcasts you will be creating something that appeals to a wide range of audiences. Create content for your current customer base as well as content which could attract new customers: this way, you are offering great value to your current customer base and still promoting your coaching business to possible newbies.

I would also recommend that you keep your postings scheduled in the same way as the newsletter. Again, this gives

Who are my different clients?

NLU every time each 1 week

your audience a certain rhythm so they start to expect to see something from you. I like to post my content on a late Sunday afternoon when people are likely to be relaxing at home and catching up on their mail and social media channels.

SOCIAL MEDIA GROUPS
General Advantages

Another dimension to social media platforms which is relevant to customer acquisition is the different types of groups which can be followed. Here you have the chance to talk and exchange with like-minded people from across the globe and share in the passion for the chosen subject.

You can follow the top coaches from your industry and join in with their conversations, and you can create your own group and share your knowledge and experience with its members. This is an excellent opportunity for any coach to promote their products and services as well as getting feedback from potential customers. If you manage to build a large following or to become an influential member of a group, then you will open new doors for business with a worldwide audience.

If you join professional groups such as those on LinkedIn you will also have direct access to some of the brightest minds in your industry, keeping you up to date with the latest trends and cutting edge technologies. I have found that by participating in these groups I have learned many new ideas, which I have then been able to turn into content for my own audiences.

Tho wasn't good I want it to be as smooth as apple i do it

ONLINE BOOKING SYSTEMS
Customer Acquisition

An online booking system is more of a convenience tool than a customer acquisition tool. Of course, if potential customers see that you have an online portal, it is attractive and shows them that you are a modern professional who has all the important tools for customer service and convenience. More or less everything we do today is digital, so having the flexibility to book courses and sessions online any time of the day or night is a great service to your current customers and any potential new ones.

I recommend that the link to this booking system can be found on all your touch points and on your business card. I have the booking link as a fixed element on my website and my regular newsletter. If a potential customer spontaneously decides to book something with you then you need them to be able to find the link address quickly and conveniently.

As a Communication Tool

An online booking system, much like an email platform, stores and collects data on your customers and automated messages can be sent out to all your users at any time. This is excellent if, for example, you suddenly see that you have some unexpected slots available and need them filling at short notice. Another useful aspect of booking systems is that reminder notifications are sent out to your customers one or two days before their lesson, reminding them of the time and place.

You are able to set your working hours, your working location and have online payments made directly to you all through your online booking system, as well as linking the platform to your email providers to create a complete customer base. You can place all your packages and courses on the platform and use it as a registration system if you want: this is a modern, efficient way of working which trumps any normal digital calendar.

COACHING PLATFORMS
Customer Acquisition

Coaching platforms are a recent addition to the sports coaches' communication strategy, but they add tremendous professionalism and value to your audience. Advertising the idea that your customers have their very own improvement space or coaching area on a specialised platform is without doubt a great selling point. The ability for you and your customers to upload data and useful media to a single platform and to share ideas is something that (at the time of writing this book) will set you apart from most of the other coaches in your region.

As a Communication Tool

In my opinion, having a dedicated coaching platform such as CoachNow or CaochHub for my customers has been one of the best investments I have made. All of my customers who use the platform enjoy uploading their own swings, sharing their data with me and receiving my recommended information. Just as with the online booking system, if I have a document or a video which I think everybody can benefit from I am able to send it to all the spaces on my platform with a single click. Both the coach and the customer receive notifications whenever something has been uploaded or has changed within a space.

The cost of coaching platforms varies but you can budget around €300 per year for a good one. I offset this cost by developing packages whereby the use of the platform is included within the price, or I charge customers a small monthly fee. Another option is to include the platform costs in your overall hourly rates: by the end of the season the coaching platform will pay for itself and even be a source of income.

Using this type of system also opens the door to other opportunities such as the long distance learning package mentioned in a previous chapter, and is very useful for coaching and managing teams.

Good idea

BLOGS, ARTICLES & VLOGS
Customer Acquisition

If you write regular blogs, articles or if you record videos on YouTube there is a good chance that many of your readers and followers are not yet your customers. Creating this type of content is an excellent way of showcasing your knowledge and character to a wider audience.

If your blogs are interesting and you are able to share relevant information with your audience then you will begin to see new faces following your channels, reading your posts and eventually turning up to your courses.

Using YouTube or any other video platform is an even more effective way of doing this, because the audience can actually see and hear you, which allows your personality and character to shine through. Video platforms are certainly growing in popularity, and many people prefer to quickly watch something rather than read it. However, I personally prefer to create both options because the demographic of my ideal customer is slightly older and they generally still prefer to read.

Another advantage of writing blogs and articles or creating videos is the accumulation of intellectual property you will have online: this will pop up any time somebody searches for you online. This leaves a positive impression on potential customers and elevates your reputation as a knowledgeable, competent coach with academic skills.

As a Communication Tool

In terms of sharing your content with your audiences and communicating with them, blogging, vlogging and writing articles are excellent strategies that can help your business to grow and expand. A modern sports coach must take advantage of these technologies in order to stay in touch with the ever-changing customer dynamic.

Creating this type of content for your customers really does add tremendous value for them, and will help to keep you and your coaching business at the forefront of their minds. I write a regular blog for my coaching business and have a YouTube channel. Both take time to manage and both need regular attention, but the rewards I receive easily outweigh the time and effort of developing content and sharing it with my audiences.

Not everybody is ready to jump in front of a camera and it does take practice to become comfortable filming yourself, so I can understand if developing videos is not something you are prepared to do. Writing down your opinions and sharing them with your audience is, simple by comparison: anybody can do it. Or, if you have subjects which need more explanation then begin to create articles with titles like "The 5 Most Important Warm up Keys" or "10 Reasons Why You Are Not improving".

PODCASTS
Customer Acquisition

A podcast is a streamed or recorded presentation the only difference with vlogging is that a podcast is only the recorded audio of the presentation. Podcasts are excellent because, much like audio books, they can be listened to while someone is commuting or travelling. If you have an interesting library of podcasts which can be downloaded by anybody, anywhere in the world, then you open the door to a much wider audience.

I personally use the audio recordings from all of my YouTube videos and release them as a podcast for my audience to listen to. A podcast could be the key to a new customer hearing your opinion for the very first time and looking further into what you do and what you offer. Naturally, having a podcast also builds upon that ever-growing intellectual property which, together with the other digital footprint methods mentioned in this book, will be becoming substantial. The more avenues via which potential customers can stumble across your work, the higher the chances are that you can add a new name to your expanding contact list.

As a Communication Tool

Using your podcast as a communication tool works very much the same as blogging and vlogging: it is a platform using which you can showcase your ideas, your personality and your character. But customers who are constantly on the go and do not have time to read blogs or watch videos might find time for your podcast, and they will appreciate having a medium which fits into their busy schedule and keeps them up to date with your latest news.

I have personally found that more people download my podcast than view my videos on YouTube, which tells me that my customers use and appreciate this means of communication.

LIVE WEBINARS
Customer Acquisition

Presenting a live webinar open to everybody is an innovative way to attract potential new customers. Using simple telecoms technology such as Zoom, GoToMeeting or even YouTube, you can air a presentation based on any subject you want to the entire world. Use social media and your other communication channels to advertise the webinar (the date, the time, and a link to join it) and then prepare to present something of great value to your audience.

If you are not used to being in front of the camera, then I recommend practising first: it is quite initially daunting to talk to your own computer screen, not knowing who is out there and who is listening. Recording versions rather than going straight to airing live is a great way to practise this method until you are ready to press the big red button and talk to the world on a live stream.

If you can encourage your current customers to share the invitation with their friends and you publicly advertise the time, date and subject across social media, then a live webinar is an excellent way to present to new potential customers. I know I am repeating myself, but here again, you must present something of genuine value to the audience, not simply a live sales pitch.

As a Communication Tool

If you have a lot of customers and you are regularly recording videos and webinars for them, then a live session is an excellent way to communicate with all your customers at once. A simple method for this is to organise a Questions & Answers webinar where you have already received maybe five to ten questions and you go about answering them live in the show. This is a great alternative to workshops if, for example, customers are stuck at home and cannot attend physical coaching sessions as may be the case in the off season periods, and have been during the Covid-19 pandemic. As an example, I organised a webinar in early 2020 for my customers covering the five biggest mistakes most amateurs make.

WHATSAPP GROUPS
As a Communication Tool

In years past, it was not socially acceptable to contact customers directly per SMS as it was thought of as being a little unprofessional. Today it is different, and setting up WhatsApp groups for your customers is a great way of communicating directly with them.

It is highly important that you have the participants' consent to add them to the group: usually, when you reassure them that the purpose of the group is to send them helpful, valuable information, they will agree to it.

I have set up numerous WhatsApp groups in my coaching business: it has become a valuable part of my communication strategy. Make sure you communicate some "house rules" for the members of the group, in order to avoid any inappropriate messages or distasteful content. WhatsApp groups are simple to set up and easy to manage, and they add a direct communication channel to your business. Do not overlook this simple method of communication for your coaching business.

FEEDBACK FORMS

One of the most under-rated but valuable sources of information is a feedback form, which can be both digital and physical. A simple feedback formula sent annually to your customers will immediately tell you what they think of the kind of services you are providing and where you need to step up your game. Make this formula a multiple choice layout, but include a comments box for those all important messages. You will be amazed at the results you receive, and possibly surprised by the opinions and thoughts of some of your customers.

The first time I did this I was completely shocked by the realisation that I really hadn't understood my customer base at all! I was filling my courses and I was busy, but it turned out that one in every five of my customers could not find a suitable course in my service package. I also learned that 60% of my customers wished to have more fitness and strategy seminars, especially in the off season, which was something I had been completely unaware of. Without criticism we cannot learn or improve, so don't be scared of the less than positive feedback you may receive: it will only help you grow in the long run.

In the world of business and coaching, if you are standing still and not improving and evolving then you are actually going backwards. Be prepared to adapt some of your courses and to cancel others. The desires and requirements of your customers are changing every season and you must step up to meet their needs in order to keep your coaching business sustainable over a long period of time.

ANALYTICS AND INSIGHTS – DIGITAL MARKETING FEEDBACK

To end this section, I want to add that all the digital communication platforms we have covered above come with excellent insight and analytics feedback tools. This is a really important part of your business because, by using these insights, you will begin to see how your customers are reacting to the content you are sending them. Without these tools it is truly difficult to know if your messages are achieving what you are setting out to achieve.

If your content and communications are useful and relevant to your audience, you will see that your emails are regularly being opened, your social media posts are being liked and shared, and the links you have inserted into posts are being clicked on. If the opposite is true then you need to think long and hard about what type of content you are producing.

This continual interaction between you and your audience is one of the keys to selling your future products and services. If you notice that your communications are falling on deaf ears then you must change your messaging in order to retain and motivate your stagnating customer base.

Now that you have some ideas and methods on how to build up your customer base, and how communication tools can help you to retain your current audience and acquire new customers, we are ready to explore the next part of maximising our income which is about how to build business and develop partnerships.

SUMMARY – CHAPTER SIX

- A modern coaching business must stay up to date with a more technologically minded customer. This means investing in modern communication tools and using the latest advanced coaching technologies is important if you wish to keep up with your competitors
- Consider modern tools such as online booking systems, coaching platforms and email marketing services, social media and websites in order to promote your products and services effectively to your customers
- Use social media platforms to promote your brand, your character and the knowledge and competence you offer
- Write blogs, articles, eBooks and other educational content to show your academic abilities and grow your intellectual property
- The simplest communications forms such as messenger, Skype, Whatsapp and email are still the most appreciated today by your customers
- Create some sort of feedback mechanisms in order to understand exactly what you are doing well and what needs to be improved
- Use the analytics and insights to measure and understand how your current communication and sales strategies are performing

7
BUILDING BUSINESS & SUCCESSFUL PARTNERSHIPS

At the time of writing, we are experiencing the second year of the Covid-19 pandemic, and it has served as a reminder that, no matter how successful we are in our businesses, the working conditions to which we have become accustomed can change in a flash. From one day to the next, it is possible that we will have no income whatsoever and that all the sports & leisure facilities will be closed down. More than ever before, it is important that your business is not reliant on only one source of income, and that it is instead well prepared to weather a storm such as the pandemic.

In 2011, I decided that the future would be more digital and enrolled in an Open University marketing degree which was followed by a master degree in digital marketing. After I qualified, I started a digital marketing agency specialising within the medical industry, together with a business partner. This was a second leg for me to stand on, just in case the first one broke! This agency is still running successfully today and gives me an interesting alternative to my coaching business as well as continued work and income, even while my coaching business is restricted to online work only.

Since then I have started multiple businesses and expanded into different fields from the sports industry. This has enabled me to increase my income but, more importantly, it has made me less reliant on my coaching business as a source of income, which is invaluable in times of trouble.

In this chapter we will touch on some of the keys to building up new businesses and outline the important rules for partnerships and alliances.

YOU PROBABLY HAVE THE SKILLS

The sports industry is a fragile one, and if you are self-employed like me, many factors can influence your ability to work and earn money. If you have other skills and qualifications then consider starting a second or third business.

I know it sounds a little crazy as a suggestion, but it isn't as difficult as you may think. What other services can you offer? What other skills do you have which can be monetised? Do you need to take further education to learn the skills which would support a passion you have? Can the new business be run from home or online? I studied and passed my qualifications while working full-time as a golf professional, by studying in the evenings and at weekends.

The second business can simply start as a side hustle until it grows into something much bigger. At that point you can decide how you want to manage it: whether you should do it alone or by employing somebody to help you with it. Many successful entrepreneurs started their businesses as something on the side while working full-time in another job then, when it grew into something bigger, they focussed more time and resources on it.

SOME GOLDEN RULES FOR STARTING A NEW BUSINESS

1. Make sure you are passionate about the industry you want to get into and happy to do the type of work it requires. If you are not passionate about the job it will feel like hard work and you will not enjoy the process and not stay committed to its success

2. Research exactly who your potential customers are and how you intend to reach out to them. Do not think for a second that you can simply set up a company and customers will immediately be knocking on your door

3. Look at which companies are already leaders in that field: what can you offer that they don't? Or is there something

that you intend to do better than your competition? Even if there is competition in your chosen field, it does not mean that there is no space for you too

4. Do not start a business which requires a huge initial investment if it is only going to be a side hustle. Research what the start-up costs will be and how much you can build for free.

5. As boring as it sounds you must set yourself small objectives such as sales targets for the short, medium and long term, customer numbers or X amount of products sold. This keeps you working towards a goal and not just aimlessly working while hoping to earn extra income

6. Ideally, set up the new company with a partner who you trust and who brings different skills to the team. Two minds are always better than one and two different skill sets really complement one another

7. Do not be frightened! It always amazes me how many people are frightened of starting a new business and are convinced it will go horribly wrong. I have started many businesses, and not all of them have been successful, but the process of making mistakes and learning from them is what makes every successful person successful in the first place! As long as you have your coaching business sustaining your income, then a side business is no great risk, especially if you have not borrowed tens of thousands to launch it

8. Never give up trying to make the business successful unless it is costing you too much money. All businesses take time to build, and they require determination and patience. Do not be deflated or de-motivated if your business does not succeed at once. Keep working on it, improving it and developing marketing channels via which you can find new customers

9. Finding a business which complements your own coaching business can really give you an advantage because you already have a happy, trusting reliable customer base you can sell your new products and services to

10. Brainstorm your business ideas and write down the advantages you will be offering to potential customers. Then send these ideas to five associates or close friends and ask them if they would purchase your product or service, and why. Then ask yourself the question whether you would buy these products and services yourself, and why? And then use the feedback to improve the entire package

BECOME SPECIALISED

If starting a completely new business is out of the question for you, then consider becoming specialised in any one part of your current industry. Most sports coaches today have a wide range of knowledge on many subjects within their sport including fitness, the mental side of the sport, nutrition, equipment, strategy and technique. In the last ten years or so in golf, we have witnessed the rapid growth of technology-based equipment which is aimed at helping us with our coaching.

For example, ballistic technology which monitors the flight of the ball for technique improvement and the fitting of new equipment is highly popular. Detailed 3D biomechanical vests and sensor systems can now record the exact movements of the body and calculate at which speed each moving part is travelling. Force plates in the ground can now record exactly what a golfer's body weight is doing during the swing as well as how much pressure they are applying into the ground. All these technologies can be explored as possible specialisation opportunities. And golf is not the only sport in which these new analytic technologies are evolving and influencing how a coach works with his or her customers.

TECHNOLOGY & SPECIALISATION

The advantage of new technologies is that you can implement them into your everyday coaching business and charge a premium rate for them, or you can become a specialist who is responsible for the technology in any given area. If you get the qualifications and build up a reputation as a specialist, customers will travel from far and wide to consult with you. What systems do you already use and are passionate about? Have you followed further education in that field? How many other coaches near you are using them? Is there a demand from your customers for these modern systems?

Be aware that some of these technologies are initially very expensive to invest in so it is crucial for you to develop a complete business plan as to how long it will take to achieve your return on investment (ROI) and begin to make a profit. If the technology is commonplace amongst coaches in your region it will be almost impossible to charge a large premium for its usage.

A friend of mine decided to become a sport Pilates coach a few years ago. Some people laughed at him, but today he earns over six figures annually, integrating his Pilates courses, weekend getaways, trips and online seminars into his coaching business on top of his everyday golf coaching services. Who is laughing now?

PARTNERSHIPS

Partnerships in business will not only help you to create another source of income, they will also help you improve your reputation and open new doors to future potential opportunities. As sports coaching covers so many aspects of your customer's lifestyle, such as equipment and travel, fashion and accessories, fitness and leisure, health and well being to name a few, there are huge partnership opportunities for you to take advantage of as a coach. Let's discuss some of the opportunities available to you and some of the key foundations of partnerships and working alliances.

WHY ARE YOU A VALUABLE PARTNER?

- You have direct access to hundreds of customers who have given you permission to write to them and advertise to them. This is something that is a valuable resource to potential partners and businesses who would normally be prevented by data protection laws from advertising directly to non customers

- You are a trusted source of information for your sporting community, and your customers respect your opinions and recommendations

- By adding new products and services to your portfolio you are adding value to your overall service package

- As you are an expert in your field you also strengthen your partners' brand reputation

- Customers of yours expect you to recommend products and services which can be beneficial for them

- You open new business opportunities and networks to your partnerships, which will help them improve their reputation within your sports community

- Many businesses have no idea about the wants and needs of non-customers, and you are the expert who can help educate your partners in the mindset and spending habits of your customer base

7 BUILDING BUSINESS & SUCCESSFUL PARTNERSHIPS

I am a Sports Ambassador for a Luxury Sports Car brand

HOW CAN YOU PROFIT?

- You will add a completely new stream of income to your coaching business by arranging commission for sales on product and services
- By partnering with trusted, renowned brands you will elevate your reputation within your sporting community
- You will open the door to completely new opportunities, business networks and potential new customers

- Depending on the contracted agreement you reach, you will probably save money on products and services provided by your partners, creating a double-win scenario
- You will be part of new events and activities which will add different experiences to your current skill set

SOME OF THE COMMON MISTAKES MADE IN BUSINESS PARTNERSHIPS

- The partner doesn't truly believe in the product and therefore does not represent the brand wholeheartedly
- The partner is not really a salesperson and is not willing to push the partner's products and make sales. Choose products you are passionate about and partners who you really support: then the sales will come from your enthusiasm. Think of it as helping your customers rather than selling to them
- Products end up being "forced" upon customers who do not require them or need them, creating a bad reputation for the coach and bad advertising for the brand
- No measurements or sales targets are agreed upon between the partners, which will monitor success of the partnership. This leads to a breakdown in trust between the two parties and the partnership ends prematurely. Always agree on exactly how the success of the partnership will be measured before signing the contract

7 BUILDING BUSINESS & SUCCESSFUL PARTNERSHIPS

- The partner misrepresents the company in a way to try and keep more income for his or herself, which in the end is always discovered and the coach loses the trust of both his or her customer base and the partner
- The partner represents too many products or too many companies at the same time, which weakens the value of their products and services and leads customers to believe their interests are no longer at the heart of things
- The company is only intent on getting direct access to the partner's customer base and is not interesting in investing time and energy in the relationship
- The partner represents products and services which are of no benefit to his or her customer base and therefore almost impossible to promote
- The partner makes impossible sales promises to the company at the outset which he or she can never achieve, leading to a breakdown of trust in the relationship between the two parties
- The partner does not actively promote the company's products and therefore is not adding value to the partnership. Define exactly what is expected from both parties and what is your role in the partnership at the beginning
- The partner only contacts the company when he or she has an invoice which needs paying. As with any partnership in life, it is important that there is ongoing dialogue between the two parties

Here are some other things to consider in business partnerships.

RELATIONSHIPS ARE GIVE AND TAKE

If you want to build sustainable long-term business partnerships they must be built on a "win win" foundation. If you are not in it for the long run, then it is not a partnership so, as with your own coaching customers you must be prepared to build a relationship with your business partners.

In my experience you must believe in the products and services you are representing, and hold your business partner's interests close at heart. If this is the case, you will have no problem recommending their products and services to your customers because you will genuinely be passionate and enthusiastic about the benefits they provide.

If everything you communicate to your customer base is simply a sales pitch, then they will start to try and avoid you and unsubscribe from your mails and newsletters. Try to see yourself as a problem solver rather than a salesperson and demonstrate how you benefit from your partner's products and services

Even if sales initially don't go well, as long as you are upholding your side of the agreement and continually working hard to promote your partner then that is OK.

BE THE ENERGY AND CREATION IN THE PARTNERSHIP

As with all successful partnerships in life, it is important to work continually on what you are bringing to the relationship. I have found that if I am continually communicating new and interesting "win win" ideas to my partners, it really strengthens the relationship between us. Do not forget that you are the expert in your field and you have the knowledge of what your customer base likes and dislikes. So, it is up to you to bring the ideas forward on how the partnership can flourish.

If you want to generate extra income, you need to be creative and proactive when it comes to proposing new ideas and activities, and never being afraid if an idea does not work. Your business partners will appreciate the energy and commitment you are bringing to the relationship, so they will generally try and support you as much as they can.

MAKE A CONTRACT

As obvious as this may sound I cannot overstate the importance of having a contract with your partner, regardless of your relationship with them. I have seen and heard so many examples of business partnerships falling apart due to the fact there was only a verbal agreement in place and not a written contract. Unfortunately the days of being able to accept a man's honest word have long gone, and you must have the entire criteria of your work together written down and signed by both parties.

This not only protects you legally but also helps you to structure the working relationship on both sides. You can sit together and discuss who is doing what and what is expected from both sides. This also gives you the option to end the business relationship if the other party is not keeping up their end of the agreement.

AN EXCELLENT CAREER DECISION

In 2009, I was fortunate to meet a new customer who was a doctor in a small private hospital in the city where I live. He told me that, together with a few of his golf-playing doctor friends and members of the physiotherapy team, they were building a golf sports clinic. The idea was to help golfers recovering from injuries or operations to safely get back into the sport through physiotherapy and injury-free technical instruction. They were also offering other services such as Pilates for golf, yoga for golf and general golf fitness check-ups.

Passionate and motivated as they were none of them were particularly good at golf, so I instantly offered my services as an expert in the field of golf. (Obviously they were all experts in their fields: sport medicine, physiotherapy and orthopaedic surgery). I told them they couldn't have amateurs trying to give technical advice to patients who may be suffering from serious injuries. I was given an interview by the team and was taken on board as the golf expert and partner.

Joining this partnership was one of the most successful decisions of my career. Not only did I start to work with new customers in a new environment but I began to do interviews for the local radio station, presentations recorded for television and to have my name featured in the local newspapers. I began to increase my income, elevate my reputation, and understand the importance of working in a medical sporting team environment. On top of that, I was given translation work to do for the doctors as I am bilingual, earning me even more income and expanding my network. This became the basis for setting up my medical digital marketing company a few years later. That entire period of my career was amazing, and I still have customers today that I met all those years ago at the private hospital.

SUMMARY – CHAPTER SEVEN

- Consider what other services you can offer in order to open another stream of income
- Start your second business as a side hustle, do not invest too much time and money into it unless you are sure it can become a serious stream of income
- Never start another business if you are truly passionate about the industry or the products and service you will provide. Be sure to research that industry and evaluate whether or not you can develop a better business than those who are already established
- If you start a joint venture with a friend or associate, then make sure your skills complement each other and that you are both prepared to work as hard as each other on making it a success
- Set yourself small manageable targets and build your business up step by step. Do not expect your new business to be an immediate success, just keep working away at it and fine tuning it until it succeeds
- Becoming specialised within your currently industry is a great way in which you can elevate your reputation and earn more income through premium services
- Develop "win, win" partnership with companies who can help you add tremendous value to your business, open new networks for you, and give you the platform to showcase yours skills and knowledge

- Never be afraid of failure, if you are committed to the process of developing your coaching business then all failures will become valuable lessons for future successes

8
GENERATING INCOME ONLINE

There is no avoiding the massive income opportunities that are available today online and the ease with which we are able to build income-creating systems, and share our knowledge with the entire world has never been so apparent. When you are building new streams of income for your coaching business, it is vital that you explore some of these new opportunities and at least develop the knowledge needed to operate some of the basic online technologies.

Just imagine that you can develop products today which can be downloaded or purchased 24 hours a day and sold to customers who live on the other side of the world and who you have never met. This was simply not possible even 15 years ago but now it is commonplace. Today you can share a piece of content that is seen instantly by tens of thousands of people and build a brand for yourself in a matter of months. As a modern sports coach hoping to increase your income and your exposure to new audiences, you need to be part of this ever-growing landscape.

In this chapter we will look at some of the online platforms you can use to monetise your knowledge and the methods of achieving this. We have looked at these in previous chapters in regards to communication, customer acquisition and retention – but now our focus is solely on how we can use these platforms to generate more income.

A PERSONAL WEBSITE – THE HUB OF YOUR SALES

One of the most common methods of selling products and services online is by using your website as the centre of all your activities. This website should be a clean-looking site which is easy to navigate and full of interesting, relevant content. The days of having to spend tens of thousands on a website are long gone and there are many service providers who will help you build a solid website at a very reasonable price.

The website should be easy to find online, which means you must implement some sort of SEO program and you must secure it using a SSL key, especially if you are taking customers payments directly on your site.

One idea is to build your website as the absolute centre or hub of all your coaching activities, meaning it should house all of your intellectual property. This means customers can visit your site and find everything they will ever need within its pages. On my website it is possible to buy products, download articles, watch videos, read my previous newsletters, book a lesson with me and subscribe to all my social media platforms.

Below is a list of potential income-generating ideas that could be placed upon your website:

- Products – All products which you sell should be listed and available on your website

- Lesson Packages – A list of all the possible coaching packages you offer along with the ability to register or order them directly online

- EBooks & Downloads – If you have digital products such as eBooks or PDFs which can be purchased by downloading them, then these should be available on your website

- Online Courses – If you have set up a library of videos or an online course which can only be accessed by payment and registration, then the sign-in and sign-up page should be available on your website

- Online Shop – If, like me, you run an online shop or have partners who have an online shop then feature the relevant page on your website or, as we'll discuss below, directly embed products to your website

- Crowd funding Platforms – If, like many coaches today, you have set up a crowd funding page to help you finance projects, then users of your website should be able to find this along with all the important information and a link for joining it on your website

- Business & Partner links – If you run other businesses and you are qualified to offer different services, it is important for you to advertise them somewhere on your website. I have a links in my footer menu which takes customers to my online shop and my digital marketing agency. Likewise, if you are advertising products and services for a partner then their website or product page should be available somewhere on your site

- Services – We talked in a previous chapter about becoming specialised or offering different services to your customers: if you can offer those other services, then advertise them on your website

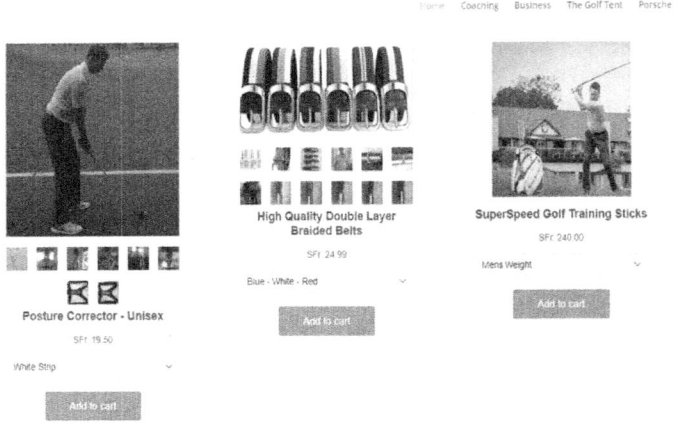

Some of my online shop products can be purchased directly from my website

INCOME FROM THE WEBSITE ITSELF

Earning income directly from your personal website is possible, but not easy. One option is to sell advertising slots to another business on your website. This is only realistic if your traffic numbers (users visiting your site) are enormous. Finding possible sponsors to sponsor your site is a quicker, easier way to directly earn income from your site, especially if you sell to a real niche market. In this case, it is realistic to agree on a yearly sponsorship fee as you can be a valuable asset for any sponsor.

You could set up a crowd funding site which allows followers, supporters and customers to donate sums of money to you on a monthly basis, helping you to complete tasks and projects. Some of this income could go towards supporting your website. In return you will need to offer your donors something of value (more on that below)

Bear in mind that search engines such as Google and Bing also have banner advertising options which allow them to place products and advertising on your website: each time a banner is clicked and a sale made, you are eligible for a small commission. However, is not very customer-focussed and, to be honest, for a professional coaching business, it does not come across very well.

ONLINE INCOME GENERATORS IN MORE DETAIL
Selling Products

One of the first methods for generating income online is to sell products. This can be done on your website or through links to another website or one of your partners. As we mentioned earlier, you will want to have any products or training aids that you use in our coaching available for purchase at any time and these should be on your website too.

It is easy and convenient to set up credit card and PayPal payment options on your website which will allow your guests to pay in complete security, and you can even automate orders so that, as they are paid for, they are distributed. You can personally stock the products you sell and then organise the distribution yourself (this is how Amazon started) or have your products stored at a global warehouse that will process the order and make the delivery for a small fee. Another method is to advertise products online and, when they are paid for, order them directly from the manufacturer and they deliver them to the customer. As mentioned earlier, this method is known as drop shipping. Selling products is a quick, easy way to boost your income and you can use the online world to facilitate the entire process.

An Online Shop

If you want to take the selling of products a little more seriously then why not open your own online shop. There are numerous platforms available online that will more or less build the entire online shop for you, leaving you to simply design the store front, stock the products and decide how you wish to have them delivered. The costs of setting up an online shop are tiny compared to renting an actual store in a commercial building.

As we discussed above, you can decide whether or not you stock the products, order them directly or have them drop shipped to the customers. I started my online shop in 2020 and, although I am a newbie, I find it very cool, and see the potential as limitless. I have decided upon a mixture of the different sales methods: some products I have designed and developed myself with my own branding and I stock them locally. Other products are ordered and paid for on my shop, and then there is an automated email which orders them directly from the manufacturer who processes the order for me and sends me a monthly invoice.

If you decide to go big on this idea and really open the doors to serious income, then companies such as Amazon offer seller programs which will stock your products for you and take over the entire sales process for a monthly fee. Obviously, if your products are advertised on Amazon with monthly traffic numbers in excess of two billion people users a month (at the time of writing) then it is likely you will make some sales.

Do not think it is easy money though, there is a lot of time and energy needed to set up the shop, order the products, advertise the products and manage the sales. But once it is running you really can earn income while you sleep. You can use all your communication channels to promote your shop or individual products and if you want more exposure then you can pay Facebook, Instagram, LinkedIn and uncle Google to promote your products for you and push traffic to your shop.

One method many successful online shops have adopted is to produce product reviews on YouTube and other social media platforms in order to help promote the products you have for sale. Some people have even earned a fortune by simply making these product reviews for other brands and being paid commission for their work.

Affiliate Income

If you do not personally want the hassle and responsibility of selling products on your website or through an online shop, then maybe an affiliate marketing program is more to your taste. This system, which is used by Amazon and most of the sales outfits in the world, pays you a commission for any leads you generate that result in a sale.

This means you can promote products on your website which have your affiliate account linked to them. If a customer clicks on that product and eventually purchases it, you will receive a commission for the sale. Obviously the commission is smaller than the profit from selling the product yourself, but you have only done a small part of the work. The affiliate option is a way of earning money without any of the risks associated with running your own shop or stocking your own products and making those product review videos or writing product review blogs will help you make sales.

This again is a method of earning extra income online while not actually working too hard for it. Remember I mentioned earlier that I built a recommended reading list for my customers and earn small commissions on the books that were purchased: it is a "win win" situation.

MONETISING BLOGS

I personally found that writing a monthly blog was a highly beneficial way of bringing web traffic to my website. Each month my blog would be sent out across all my communication channels to my audiences and numbers visiting my site would always spike. Within the pages of my blogs there are always products advertised or recommendations for my customers. Of course the main purpose of the blog is to inform my customers about what I am doing and what new plans I have, as well as giving them advice and tips for their golf games.

Whatever recommendations I gave were always linked to an affiliate account (most large ecommerce platforms have an affiliate marketing program which you can sign up to for free). As long as you keep these affiliate accounts open you will still be earning commission on those recommendations years down the line. Be aware, however, that some links will be changed by the affiliate company and you must check from time to time if your affiliate link is still working or not and amend it to the appropriate product.

Blogs are a great way to showcase your personality and help readers get to know you better. Even if the blog doesn't directly earn you money through product placement, it will help you gain new customers and help you sell other products and services.

Again if you have a huge blog following then finding a sponsor should be the next step to monetising your blog. Businesses love websites that have huge visitor traffic volumes and they are ready to splash the cash to advertise to your audience. This sponsorship money, on top of the affiliate products sales can be an excellent way to generate a high income through blogging.

My personal blog with an affiliate recommended reading list link to Amazon

CREATE EBOOKS

You may be reading this as an eBook right now. If so, you will know that you had to purchase it just like a book from a store (hopefully it has been worth it). If you like writing and have enough information to write an eBook then why not do it. A book is an excellent product to have, the costs involved are a lot less than having a book physically published and you can fill it with links to other pages. Maybe you have a collection of blog posts or some short stories which could be made into an eBook. Or maybe, like me, you have a lot of ideas about your industry which you want to share with the world.

As soon as an eBook is finished it is ready for download, and once placed on your website or maybe in your shop it is there to earn income for you 24 hours a day, even while you sleep! If it becomes hugely popular then have it translated into other languages and maybe even update it every few years to keep it fresh.

Audiobooks

I am a huge fan of audiobooks and listen to one every time I step into my car or have to travel somewhere. For me, they are the simplest way to gain knowledge while on the go. If you have written a book or an eBook then consider making an audiobook version of it. You can narrate it yourself or have somebody else do it: either way, it is an excellent income generator for content you have already created.

Audiobooks can be purchased and downloaded by all major music and entertainment platforms and can be promoted through all your other social media channels, I believe they will become even more popular in the future as more and more commuters latch onto the idea of listening and learning while on the move.

Podcasts

Much like audiobooks, a podcast is an audio presentation which can be listened to on the go or while relaxing at home, the difference being that podcasts are usually shorter presentations similar to those on YouTube and are often a weekly or monthly series. Most podcasts are actually free of charge, but if you have a very large following or offer something exclusive like education or consultancy within your podcast, you can charge to download them.

I run a podcast which is simply the audio recording of my YouTube channel: it is intended for those customers of mine who do not have time to watch my videos but want to keep up with my content. This content is free and is used as a base for selling and promoting other products and services.

Online Courses

If you have enough interesting content to fill an entire course then maybe setting up an online course for customers is an option that could earn income for you. There are numerous ways in which you can do this, from simple webinars as part of a series to pre-recorded videos which are only available for users who have paid a fee and been given a sign-in username and password.

Maybe you have already covered multiple themes as presentations with your customers and wish to turn these into an online course, or you decide to start at the very beginning and build a ten-part series. You can do this through a combination of PowerPoint presentations, videos and live broadcasts or simply record your content with a voiceover. There is some preparation time associated with these types of courses but you can budget that into the overall cost of the course: you will also need some of those communication technologies we discussed earlier, like Skype or Zoom.

During the first lockdown I offered my customers a six-part online course covering the basics of the mental game in golf. I had eight paying participants who received a zoom link from me once a week. We went through a PowerPoint presentation together for 90 minutes and it worked really well. I also sent them all some old material of mine, from previous golf psychology courses, and amended it to fit this course so they could fill in the answers themselves each week.

This course can now be used over and over again: it will also be a product which I can amend and improve on. Once you have created a course of some sort it can also be printed off and used offline for group seminars or one-to-one courses.

Educational Articles & Curricula

We discussed writing articles for magazines or newspapers as a potential source of income in a previous chapter and, of course, that is also relevant for online income. If you have written tons of blogs and articles or you have offered several online courses and lessons then why not consider writing an educational course or coaching curriculum for an association or school.

Every association is looking to modernise the education they are providing to their members and they are always on the lookout for new material. Even a company who produces educational material for the public is in need of new interesting content and your course could be what they are looking for.

I know of other coaches in the world of beauty and wellbeing who write curricula for online schools and universities and are paid a lot of money to do it. If you have already released an eBook or had a coaching book published then maybe breaking down the content into manageable parts for a course could be an excellent avenue for doubling up on the potential income of that material.

Live Webinars

Before the Covid-19 pandemic, some of the top coaches who have a large following were organising special "one off" webinars which required a small entrance fee to participate. With the online webinar trend becoming commonplace due to the effects of working from home and teachers no longer being able to present live to crowded conference rooms, the chances of charging for a webinar have actually decreased.

We have seen many of the top coaches worldwide participating more and more often in free live webinars, as a way of expressing solidarity with and helping other coaches who are stuck at home or with no current income.

But if you organise a live webinar for your customers and it gives them the ability to learn from the comfort of their homes then there is still no reason why you cannot charge a small entry fee. You can regulate this by only sending the log in details to those who have already paid the fee.

Long Distance Coaching Packages

If you have already purchased a coaching platform (see the communication tools chapter) then you can begin to offer services which were unthinkable ten years ago. One such service is a long distance coaching package aimed at anybody, anywhere in the world. I already mentioned the gentleman I met while playing golf in Miami, who went on to become my student over the long distance platform.

This is a great example of a source of income that I had not expected and definitely something to consider for any coaching business. Some of your students may have moved away but would love still to have your help or maybe you have regional or national players who travel a lot, so you need a 24/7 system which can accommodate your coaching relationship with them. Offering some sort of long distance learning program or course opens your coaching business to the entire world and develops another new potential stream of income.

Crowdfunding Platforms

If you already have a substantial customer base and you are developing new projects, like finishing a book, or building an application for the iPhone or Android, then a crowdfunding platform might be useful to you. Put simply, a crowdfunding platform allows people to donate money to help support you and your business objectives. Some of these donations are simply charitable acts of kindness, made because the donor likes you, while others are returned in the form of products and services or special discounts and exclusive content.

If you able to build a large crowd of supporters all contributing money on a monthly basis to your projects then this can be an excellent source of income. Just be aware it is not "free" money and you will have to regularly show them where their investment is going and make it worth their while with valuable services and products in return. You can set the minimum and maximum donations and use your communication platforms to explain exactly how it is helping you. This crowd sourcing method is a fascinating way of getting financial support from your audience without directly selling them any particular service or product. Those coaches who run such schemes are high value coaches who are willing to put in a lot of work in order to repay the support of their customers. Do not consider this idea if you cannot produce the value in return.

Using Paid Advertising to Promote and Sell

Any activity online whether it is using SEO tools to help you build up your website traffic or social media channels to sell products, can be enhanced through the use of paid advertising. All the major players in the online scene allow you to place advertisements and create promotion campaigns: at a cost. You can decide how much you wish to budget for on a daily, weekly or monthly basis and your adverts will be seen by audiences beyond your current followers and sphere of influence.

The campaigns can be made up of target audiences like friends of friends or they can focus on large cities and specific demographics. You will see an estimated audience exposure number based on how much you are willing to spend and the keywords you have picked out for the target audience. Obviously the more money you spend the more exposure your campaign will have, and the higher the chance is that you can successfully promote your products or services.

Make sure that all your paid advertising campaigns have some sort of call to action within them. This means a link to a site or product page, or even just the ability to like, follow and share. The audience must have some sort of instruction as to what you want them to do when they see your adverts. Social media advertising is good value for money at the time of writing meaning you can reach thousands of potential new customers for your products and services with very reasonable base costs.

Google adverts and the like are a little more expensive and you need to use well thought out keywords to get your products and services seen on search engines. If you do manage to get your products and services listed on the first page of a search engine then it means literally tens of thousands of potential customers will see your promotion.

One of the great advantages of all digital advertising on social media or with search engines is the insights and analytics tools you can use to see exactly how effective you're advertising campaigns are and how many people have seen them. Let us say that your campaign target was to increase traffic numbers to your website or to a certain page on your website. Using the insights and analytic feedback tools you will be able to see exactly how many people did indeed visit your website and their behaviours while on your site, for instance: did they visit other pages; did they click on certain products; how long did they actually spend on your site; and which device were they using. These kinds of key metrics give you feedback as to what needs to be done in order to achieve your objectives and how you can improve your site or product page to increase sales or achieve whatever your goal is.

I have experienced an unbelievable increase in visitor traffic numbers to my website by using paid advertising but the key then is to capture the visitors and funnel them to some sort of purchase, if that was the goal of your campaign. Make sure you do not go crazy spending thousands on advertising if you do not have the funnelling systems and the products in place and available to purchase.

GENERATING INCOME THROUGH SOCIAL MEDIA

Although social media is in its infancy as a technology we all know how big and how important it has become as a platform to grow a brand, sell products and share information. This trend will certainly continue for a long time to come and if you want to open new streams of income online then we cannot overlook its importance.

In this section we will look at some of the key social media platforms and discuss ways to earn income from them. I am personally not a social media expert and use them much more for communication and the growth of my personal brand then directly as a source of income. However I can share with you many ideas I have seen or that have been used by other coaches to boost their income.

Facebook

Facebook is generally considered today to be an older person's social media platform, which is great if you are a golf coach like myself because the average demographic of my customers is 40 years old and more and this is the Facebook generation.

Facebook is very good site for advertising your products and services and engaging your audience to read and watch your content. Consider creating a business page, a product page and a fan page to build up your Facebook following. Then develop and share interesting content which is of value to your audience and set up a group via which you can talk with your followers. The aim is to create conversations and interact with your audience in order to help build up a relationship with them. If you really want customer engagement, ask questions, comment on their points, organise quizzes and give away prizes.

If you build a faithful group of followers then you will find it quite easy to sell your products and services to them. If you manage to get especially high numbers of followers you may want to consider the affiliate marketing idea we discussed above, which does not take a lot of work to set up and can be profitable.

If you sell products directly or have an online shop then I would strongly recommend integrating a product page to your Facebook account and investing in Facebook adverts to promote and sell them. I know that 80% of the sales from my online shop come through advertising on Facebook and by boosting product-related posts.

If you really step up the numbers and become an influencer you will have Facebook supporting you financially and companies knocking down your door to help them promote their products. Some of the top coaches in the world have developed this type of following and can influence the purchasing decisions of their fans through reviewing and recommending products and services.

Some businesses are also desperate to get the number of "likes" on their own pages up, and are willing to pay influencers huge sums of money to help them achieve this. If you are personally creating tons of traffic then you hold the power to send them to any site you desire and that can be attractive to big companies.

LinkedIn

LinkedIn is much more of a business and networking platform for professionals as opposed to Facebook and Instagram, which are more about personal stories. LinkedIn is commonly used to expand one's professional network and get in touch with key influential people. As you are a professional sports coach, you belong here too. And if, like me, your customer demographics are businessmen and businesswomen, they will probably be using the network and reading your content.

Be careful here not to simply spam LinkedIn with your sales and promotions. Always consider what value you are bringing to the conversation and whether or not somebody watching will appreciate your professional opinion or not. Never forget that your reputation is on the line, especially on this platform. Keep your profile up to date and really show your audience who you are, what qualifications you have and the skills you can bring to any business.

LinkedIn also has the group options and paid advertising functions which, much like Facebook, can be used to share knowledge and build your reputation. I have personally found LinkedIn advertising to be a little more expensive than other platforms and more orientated towards big businesses.

Of course you can still promote your products and services on LinkedIn and use affiliate links in your content to earn income, but do not let it become a constant sales pitch or your audience will turn off. I think LinkedIn is best used to expand your network, showcase your knowledge and skills as a top coach and promote your content. If you offer other services, then LinkedIn is a great place to find new contacts and customers, and even to reach out to head-hunters looking for your skills.

I have personally found that the more active I have been on LinkedIn, the more businesses and professionals have reached out to me for business collaborations. If you build a network of trusted professionals, you will begin to see an increase in interactions with your posts and new opportunities which you could have never foreseen.

YouTube

If your aim is to expand your audience, build up your reputation and promote your products and services, then

YouTube is an excellent platform with unlimited earnings potential. There are different ways in which you can leverage it for your business success: how you should use it depends on what kind of role you want to play in the content produced.

It takes guts and character to step out in front of the camera and show the world exactly who you are, but if you are prepared to offer good value content and invest time and effort into your videos then there can be huge financial gains. If you prefer to stay out of the limelight, then you can always produce videos and edit a voiceover to them, so you are in the background rather than directly in front of the camera.

YouTube will financially reward you if your videos become popular and you build a large following. Like the other platforms mentioned, you have the potential to earn income through affiliate marketing, product reviews and promoting and selling your own products.

Another way of generating income is to allow other businesses to sponsor your episodes or the entire channel, allowing them to present something within your video. This might be a logo within the videos or a dedicated 30-second recommendation of their products and services.

Another popular income generator for channels who have large audiences on YouTube is members only content which requires payment for access and is not available for non-members. This can be followed by officially branded merchandise available for sale on the channel: and you can even charge followers to have their comments highlighted in the comments sections (this is known as the super chat and super sticker options). Naturally, any products and services reviewed or discussed within an episode must have some sort of link your audience can use to purchase them should they want to.

If you personally sell products or wish to promote the products of a sponsor, then I would recommend making product review videos for your audience. This is a quick, easy way into earning income from YouTube and you can build up a following very quickly. Test and review products and invite opinions and feedback from your audience. If you are well respected and trustworthy your audience will purchase the products you have reviewed.

My YouTube channel is part of my overall service package. It is intended to give coaches advice and help for their businesses. I don't primarily treat it as a source of income, as it is more about sharing my knowledge and helping others. However, such is the nature of YouTube and its power that businesses want to be involved and to support these projects.

Instagram

Much like YouTube, Instagram offers you tremendous income potential if you can build a dedicated following and influence their spending habits. This short video and picture platform works by adding key hashtags which alert users to your posts. The more specific and relevant the hash tag is, the more likely it is to attract the right audience.

Becoming an influencer is one way of earning money on Instagram which will have businesses and sponsors scrambling over themselves to pitch their products and services within your content. If you promote products within your stream then you will be paid directly by Instagram, much like YouTube.

This can be achieved through affiliate links or direct payments by a business to promote a certain product. If you have your own products or an online shop then Instagram is a great way to promote your products and get traffic visiting your chosen website. Facebook owns Instagram, so most advertising campaigns can be managed through your Facebook account. I have also found that businesses will reach out to you on Instagram if they see you are getting good traction or you have an interesting product.

There are many methods by which you can build up a large following and start to earn income on Instagram, but always remember it is your reputation on the line and offering genuine, relevant content which helps solve someone's problem, whether it is through advice or a product, will always be a strong, sustainable strategy in the long term.

CONCLUSION

Regardless of which platforms you decide to use, social media and the online realm give you the opportunity to build a brand as big as you want. All of these avenues take time and knowledge to develop and focussing on any one of them will potentially increase your income. Decide what kind of content you are prepared to produce and how much time you are able to invest in content development. Once you have found an avenue that excites and motivates you, choose the platform which is best suited to you.

Use social media primarily as a communication source. This will increase your follower numbers and help present you to a wider audience. Then begin to promote your products and services or the products and services of an affiliate or sponsor. As you grow your platforms, look for a sponsor who is interested in jumping on board with you. Then if you start to get very big, the social media platforms will reach out to you and help you monetise your content.

My personal opinion of the ever-changing environment of these platforms is that everything is heading in the video format direction. Even Instagram, which started as a picture only platform, is now encouraging short videos (reels), and Facebook, Snapchat and TikTok are crammed with video content. I think videos are the future. I also strongly believe in audiobooks and podcasts. They are relatively new formats when it comes to content sharing online, but they fit in to the ever busier lifestyles of your potential customers.

SUMMARY – CHAPTER EIGHT

- Taking advantage of online opportunities can dramatically increase your revenue potential, while communicating to a wider audience
- Look at any avenue that you can offer your customers great value and in return increase your income, such as crowd funding platforms, audio book and podcast channels, membership schemes and loyalty clubs
- Consider which types of products and services you can sell online, and choose the appropriate digital platform to promote them
- Use social media platforms as the voice of your brand and funnel followers to product pages
- Products and services are the quickest and most popular digital products to sell online
- Selling your knowledge as a consultant or problem solver is another idea to boosting your income online
- Education courses, webinars and eBooks / articles can also be sold online to help you promote your coaching business and build your brand
- Harness the power of paid advertising to boost your promotional activities and showcase your products and services to a wider audience
- Build specific advertising campaigns, to promote products and services or direct traffic to a designated webpage

9
BECOME A KEY PERSON OF INFLUENCE

We have discussed many methods by which a modern day sports coach can increase his or her income using the strategies and technologies outlined in this book, but one really important thing which cannot be overlooked is the fact that across all industries, the biggest income and business opportunities always land at the feet of the key persons of influence.

When you become a key person of influence within your industry, top companies and other influential individuals seek you out to help them with their income-generating projects. They request your opinions and thoughts on their ideas and they need your network and knowledge to help them achieve their goals. These business opportunities simply do not exist for individuals who are relatively unknown within an industry. And, unless you have begun to implement some of the intellectual property methods within these pages, nobody outside your circle of customers will have heard of you.

There is no one way to become a key person of influence within your industry but there are some common pathways which most key influencers have taken. In this chapter we will look at some of the ideas which will quickly elevate you and your reputation above that of a normal everyday sports coach and help you begin your journey to becoming a key person of influence.

ASSOCIATE YOURSELF WITH THE BEST COACHES

One of the quickest and most effective ways coaches become renowned and respected within their industry is by association. This means associating yourself and working together with some of the top coaches in your industry. You may want to organise a course, seminar or event at your facility and invite a renowned coach to spend time with your customers. This will be beneficial to your audience, but also open up a new working relationship with a key person of influence. Yes, some of the top coaches are extremely expensive to hire for a day or two, but we all have customers who would be willing to pay a premium to learn from the very top coaches. You can build in a small income to the event so that your organisation and initiative is paid for, and you are also certain to pick up some new email addresses for your customer base when organising these kinds of events.

This method not only offers your customers an excellent opportunity to learn from the very best, but also elevates your reputation as somebody who rubs shoulders with the very top coaches in the business.

If you are not able to organise such an event then see if it is possible to visit an influential coach with a group of your customers at his or her venue. You can build this into one of your packages whereby you spend a day or two away from your facility, practicing and learning from a renowned coach, thus adding tremendous value to your service package.

Other ways you can associate yourself with top coaches are by attending their seminars and events, registering yourself for self-improvement and spending time with a top coach working on your own game, then sharing the entire experience with your customers. Maybe you could interview a top coach by video or in person and record it as content for your audience. Or simply volunteer to spend a day with an influential figure and record the entire experience to share with your customers.

Whichever methods you choose to follow, make it one of your business objectives to spend time with and learn from the top coaches within your industry. Reach out to them and tell them that you want to improve your knowledge. Ask if they would consider helping you or being part of something you are organising. You might be surprised how open and accessible they actually are. This is because many of them climbed the ladder of influence using the same methods, and they are also always on the lookout for new collaborations and sources of income.

WRITE ARTICLES, BLOGS AND BOOKS

I cannot overstate the importance of this method when looking to build your reputation and climb the ladder. We mentioned above that writing a regular blog, creating interesting articles, producing books and eBooks are a sure way of earning more income as a modern day sports coach.

If however you are not able to monetise your knowledge in this way then do not worry, because every time you write a piece of educational content, you will be seen by your community as a knowledgeable expert who is in the know on latest topics and trends and has useful information to share. More or less all of the key persons of influence across all industries write journals, blogs and articles for magazines and many go on to produce bestselling books. Building up your (IP) intellectual property is a foundation for becoming influential within your industry. As long as your content is useful, relevant and you are giving value to your audience it will always be well received.

If you can successfully build up your IP and begin to make a name for yourself as a go-to person on important issues within your industry then new income opportunities will be just around the corner.

CREATE PARTNERSHIPS WITH REPUTABLE COMPANIES

As I mentioned, in 2011 I was asked if I would become part of a medical clinic who wanted to build a team of experts catering for injured golfers. The Hirslanden Group, who have hospitals all over the world, were planning to develop a golf clinic within their hospital in Basel. They already had orthopaedic doctors, experts in sports science and physiotherapists. They wanted to add a golf expert to the team. This partnership catapulted me to regional recognition, with public presentations to over 100 people, TV and radio appearances and, through my "one-to-one" swing checks, a new stream of customers and income. Even today, ten years later, I still coach students who I met through that work. This experience showed me the importance of creating partnerships in order to take a step up the ladder of influence within my coaching region. And it became the base for all my partnership endeavours ever since.

We discussed the potential income advantages of partnerships in Chapter 6 and we also noted the impact it has on your reputation if you align yourself with reputable companies. When you begin to represent renowned companies then your audience see that you are trusted and respected by other professionals, and this elevates your standing compared to a coach who doesn't have partnerships. A top company will not invest time and money in a partner who is not able to represent the brand, and your audience understand this.

By associating yourself with top companies and representing their products and services you will boost your reputation and take another step up the influence ladder, especially if you are able to pass advantages directly on to your own customers. I am very fortunate to represent one of the top sports car manufacturers in the world and I take my role as a sports ambassador very seriously. This role has opened many new doors of opportunity for me and I have made new contacts through the joint activities and events we have organised together.

JOIN NETWORKING GROUPS, CLUBS & SOCIETIES

In order to boost your income on top of the actual day-to-day methods described in this book, you need to expand your network and your horizons. I already recommended that you join online groups and societies to share your knowledge and opinions with a wider audience. We looked in detail at Facebook and LinkedIn, and of course there are other social media outlets such as Twitter which are excellent for this purpose.

A disadvantage of online groups is that you cannot be there in person, unless all communications are via a video or telecoms call, which still is not the same as genuinely meeting the person. A better option when trying to build up your influence is to join offline business groups and societies (if covid-19 ever allows us to again). This is where real business opportunities lie and if you can become a key member of your group then you can take advantage of them. Think of groups such as business groups, entrepreneur groups, networking societies, small business owner clubs, or clubs and groups which you think may house influential people such as wine clubs, whisky societies, cigar groups or fraternities which bring people together who share a joint passion. Of course, only join these groups if you genuinely share the specific passion they represent: never join them solely to sell yourself to the members. This will close doors rather than open them for you.

If you join many groups on and offline and you begin to make a positive impression within them, you will start to see new business opportunities come your way. We all understand the importance of networking and the effect it has on our potential business opportunities, and if you can join groups which are both fun to participate within and help you expand your business horizons, then it is a "win win" for you.

BUILD YOUR OWN GROUP

If joining other groups and networks is not really your thing, or you do not have access to the type of societies you are passionate about then consider starting your own business group. It is said that we are heavily influenced by the people around us and we can only expand our minds if the influential people around us are just as ambitious. I really believe in this principle and will discuss it again later when we talk about finance and spending habits.

Create your own group of like-minded coaches or businesspeople with the aim of regularly sitting together and exchanging ideas. Brainstorming ideas could well open the door to great new business ventures but will also help you share your ideas with a group who can give you honest and critical feedback. If we are honest with ourselves, we all believe our own ideas are good ones, but quite often nobody shares the same enthusiasm. Constructive but critical feedback from a group of trusted friends and business associates is the best way to really decide whether or not your latest, greatest idea is any good.

Spend time with like-minded individuals and you will begin to see how your mind opens to completely new opportunities that you had never thought of, and how you begin to think on a completely new level. This endeavour can only help build your knowledge and increase the likelihood that you become a person of influence.

PROVIDE EDUCATIONAL COURSES & SEMINARS

We have already highlighted the potential of earning more income through online courses and providing educational content, but the other upside to this is the way it enhances your reputation and opens new doors to business opportunities. It was because I was writing this book that I was asked by the SWISS PGA (Professional Golfers Association) to present some of my ideas to my fellow coaches as part of a further education webinar. This webinar was well received and two coaches asked me for private support for their businesses. So, one piece of educational material led me to other business opportunities: and I am sure that this book will lead me to more.

If you are producing educational material as discussed in chapter 8 and selling it to associations for their curricula then you really will be on the way to becoming a key person of influence. Whenever content is used as part of a national or international education curriculum the author of the material is requested to make presentations, give speeches and make appearances all over the world to represent his or her work. You would think this method is impossible or that the market is already saturated but do not underestimate this avenue to climbing the ladder of influence because, let's face it, how many people do you know that are writing educational material for schools and associations? Someone has to do it, and it might just be you.

BECOME SPECIALISED

If there is a certain segment of your coaching industry that really excites you and motivates you to discover more, then consider becoming specialised in that subject. In golf, for example, there have been many new, exciting niche markets within the industry over the last 10 to 15 years, mainly due to advances in technology and our knowledge in sports biomechanics. We have technology available now which gives us much more of an understanding of the way our body creates speed and exactly what causes the golf ball to fly and spin.

Through these new technologies and the expertise to implement them into everyday tuition, sports coaches have become specialised and have build up reputations as experts on their chosen subject, increasing their influence and opening new streams of income.

Whenever you are considering specialising in a technology or segment of your industry, look around first and see whether it will really add value to your service portfolio and help you stand out from your local competitors or not. If not, then it could be a lot of time and energy invested with little or no ensuing competitive advantage.

FURTHER EDUCATION

Any successful person will tell you that one of the keys to success is continued learning and self development, and I am a very strong believer in it. If you are not moving forwards then you are actually going backwards. Whatever qualifications you may have, regardless of your knowledge and your success up to now, you must keep learning and developing yourself. I have found throughout my career that there is a direct collation between how much I learn and how successful I have become and I do not think it is simply a coincidence.

I listen to audiobooks daily and participate in one or two further types of education every year. This has opened so many new doors for me and has become the base for much of the content within this book. When I decided to make education and self development a key part of my coaching strategy, I felt empowered and energised. The more I learnt, the more I could share with my audiences and the more value they would get from me and my business. Learn across a wide spectrum of subjects and you will see new angles to how you can be more successful in your life. It will also prompt you to seek out the masters of your industry and understand what they all have in common.

Make further education as important as fitness and healthy eating in your lifestyle, if you have tremendous knowledge in multiple areas and subjects the people around you will notice it, and begin to see you as a person of influence who is worth investing time and money into. I have heard people tell me that they do not have time to participate in further education due to their stressful lifestyles, family and work, but funnily enough they have the time to watch two hours of Netflix most evenings and sport at the weekends. Imagine, if just one of those hours was set aside daily for further education and self development, what the potential output could be. It is not for everyone but it is for the successful ones!

If you are constantly collecting certificates and education make sure your audience and customers hear about it. They will appreciate that you are still learning and going above and beyond what any normal coach does. Further education is one of the foundations for becoming a key person of influence, and one that will dramatically expand your income horizons.

I am still participating in further educations and trying to improve my knowledge

KEEP YOUR PROFILES UP TO DATE

When you begin to invest time and energy into some of the strategies we have outlined in this book, you will begin to see more and more people viewing your online profiles and requesting some of your time. This is good news as customers and businesses always gravitate to people who are active and making things happen.

Make sure that all your digital touch points and profiles are up to date and that all your current projects and certificates of education can be seen by any potential visitor. Your profile pages will be the first port of call for any company looking for more details on you and your coaching business.

If you are actively showing the world that you are moving in a positive direction and that your business is becoming more and more popular, the queue of people wanting to be involved with you will also keep growing. If, however, your profile pages are still, you have no new activity and show no signs of growth and success, business opportunities could well pass you by.

I do not mean that you have to go ultra Instagram and post every move you make to show the world how amazing you are and how much money you are earning, because that will only damage your reputation. But make sure all your important contact information is up to date, show a timeline of your recent posts and provide links to websites and channels you own. Make sure any visitor to your profile page can build a complete overview of all the wonderful things you are doing.

STEP BY STEP

The thought of implementing everything we have covered so far in this book can be a little bit overwhelming. However, do not lose hope or believe for a second that everything needs to be done immediately.

Try to prioritise your list of things to do: which tasks will help you immediately earn more income? Which ones will help you quickly increase your customer numbers? And which tasks will take longer to achieve but will have a long term effect on your business? One great way to measure this is by giving each task a 1-5 scale for difficulty, importance and immediate impact on your business (1= Not Very & 5= Very).

Look at the example below:

Task: Set up a Spring Course Program

Difficulty–2(easy)
Importance– 5 (very)
Impact – 5 (very immediate)

Score – 12 / 15 – Very much worth doing

Task: Build a Tips & Advice Page on my Website

Difficulty – 3
Importance – 2
Impact – 2

Score – 7 / 15 – Definitely not a priority

So here are two tasks which could be done for your coaching business but very clearly the first one, with a score of 12 / 15 is the priority. Any tasks that score high on your list are your priority, because they are important and have an immediate impact on your business regardless of their difficulty level. If the difficulty level is high but the importance and impact not, then you have to ask yourself whether or not the task is really worth doing.

This system has helped me prioritise my workload for years: and time I come up with an idea for my business I do this simple calculation. By doing this you will not waste time and energy on developing ideas which do not have a real positive impact on your business. You can of course change the three areas of criteria to something like importance, time and income generation or difficulty, time and estimated value to the business.

MENTORS & ACCOUNTABILITY

We all need support and advice to achieve successful things in life, and building a successful coaching business is no different. If, like me, you are self-employed and work more or less as a one man band, you might believe you have to do absolutely everything yourself in order to achieve your goals. I can tell you now this is not the case.

I have been very fortunate in my career to have surrounded myself with some innovative and forward thinking businessmen and women who have helped me tremendously, shaping the entrepreneur that I am today. Through watching them and listening to them and combining this with my own collection of knowledge and experiences, I have been able to see what it takes to build successful businesses and get an insight into the type of character it takes.

Try to find yourself a mentor who has successfully built businesses or who was successful in their own careers. This person must be ready to share their knowledge and knowhow with you and help support, motivate and challenge you and your ideas. A mentor keeps you on track when your energy and motivation levels are dwindling and they are there to help you overcome difficult changes that you may face. It is a difficult road to navigate when you are alone self-employed businessperson and we all fall down sometimes. This is the nature of the beast: we need these mistakes and bad experiences to learn and become successful and it is a lot easier to get back on the right track when you have a support system around you.

If no mentor is available then join an accountability group full of budding entrepreneurs like you who understand exactly the type of difficulties you are experiencing and have a wealth of knowledge and experience to put things right. Accountability groups are also excellent at keeping you on schedule and helping you finish projects you have started. Anybody can come up with great ideas, but seeing them through to the very end takes energy, determination and discipline, which a mentor or an accountability group will hold you too.

We know that being an influential figure in your field will open new doors for business and create big income opportunities. Influencers on social media, television or in the world of business are always the key drivers of innovation and change within their industries and the individuals all others look up to. Begin your journey now up that ladder of influence. Become a source of information and value and determine how far you want to go in order to maximise your income and set yourself apart from your competition.

SUMMARY – CHAPTER NINE

- Associate yourself with the top people within your industry and coordinate events and activities with them
- Produce academic material such as articles, blogs, eBooks and books to elevate your reputation and share your knowledge
- Offer educational material, courses and webinars to your fellow professionals and association to position yourself as a key person within your industry
- Develop partnerships and working alliances with reputable companies in order to elevate your reputation, open news streams of income and communicate to a new audiences
- Join or create business groups and societies in which likeminded professionals can meet, discuss and network to the benefit of all involved
- Consider becoming specialised in an area within your industry, building up a reputation as the "go to" person for that subject
- Continue your own personal development by participating regularly in further education and increasing your wider business knowledge
- Join accountability groups who help you to turn ideas into finished projects and help you widen your own professional network
- Find successful mentors who are willing to support your growth and share their knowledge and experience with you to help you become more successful

10
MONEY MATTERS

Understanding how to make money work for you and knowing the basics of wealth creation is where you can begin to really up the stakes in terms of income generation. If your vision is to work less hours and earn more income, or to work in a style that energises and motivates you, then building wealth will take some of the pressure off. It can take you away from having to do a nine-to-five day to pay for your lifestyle.

Earning a higher income is not just about creating wealth and the most successful businesspeople understand how to manage their money in order to create everlasting wealth. I am not a financial advisor nor am I a multi-millionaire: my aim here is not to tell you exactly what you should do with your income. Everyone is responsible for their own financial decision making. I would, however, like to share with you some of the key lessons I have learnt on my journey and some of the advice I learned from years of studying wealth management books, which helped me turn my money management around.

MY OWN MONEY STORY

In my early days as a golf coach I worked very long hours and often six or seven days a week. This gave me a good income and I enjoyed my lifestyle very much, going out for dinners, weekend breaks and buying myself clothes and golf equipment. However I wasn't a big spender and never blew my money on silly things, plus I lived in very cheap accommodation and drove a small economical car.

The money that I would accumulate throughout the season would almost see me through the winter months, but generally I began the next season with almost nothing in the bank, credit card debts and worried about paying any new or unexpected bills. As the season kicked off I would be OK again and pay off my debts and begin a new cycle. After four years of absolutely working my butt off, I had nothing to show for it but the normal cycle of debt and recovery.

Today I am very fortunate to have multiple businesses, properties, investments and money invested in my retirement: and none of that would have been possible if I hadn't begun to educate myself in the ways of money and how to make it work for me. It takes courage to look at yourself in the mirror and admit that change is needed to build a better future. If you are not great at managing your money then the lessons below will help you to understand how I turned things around.

Reduce Your Spending

Reducing your spending seems entirely logical when it comes to looking at your finances and trying to see where you can save money. However, most people who stay poor are reluctant to change or reduce their current creature comforts. Everybody can save a little money somewhere if they really want to. I made a note of every penny I spent for a month, every coffee, sandwich, beer and restaurant bill as well as petrol, and my normal fixed bills. Then I marked off the ones which can be classed as unavoidable, like my health insurance, my car and petrol (as I needed a car to get to work), my rent and electricity, mobile phone and so on. Then I was left with the nice-to-haves costs: yes, I needed food but I realised I was spending a lot of money in restaurants, on drinks, coffee and sandwiches all which were avoidable or could be hugely reduced. I also had a cable television subscription which I never used and was buying new golf equipment once a year which I did not really need. All of these expenses, plus my taxes were keeping me poor even though my annual income was adequate.

If you are living on the limit from one pay check to the next you are actually one step away from bankruptcy and ruin. If you want to live the lifestyle of somebody rich but you have no passive income, no savings and no investments then you will always be poor, like I was. I needed to take a long hard look at my lifestyle and be honest with myself: did I really need to live like I did, or did I want to become successful? So I reduced all the unnecessary expenses in my life to free up more of my income and begun to build wealth.

DIVIDE YOUR INCOME

Once I had addressed my crazier spending habits, I saw a little more money in my bank account at the end of every month. Next I decided to divide my money up in different money pots. Firstly, before anything was paid I put 10% of my income into a savings account. Then I opened a pension account and set up an automated transfer into that account, which was very little at the beginning but it soon starts to add up. This process is actually about building the habit of saving money, which is initially more important than the amount. Then I took a third of what was left over and put it in another account for my taxes.

Then of course I had to cover my fixed costs, which took up most of the rest of the money. I did however decrease these costs by changing to cheaper car insurance, a cheaper telephone provider and cancelling that television subscription which I hardly ever used.

I also used the money that was left over more intelligently by shopping for more cost-effective food eating more often at home, rather than at a restaurant, and taking packed lunches to work with me. Believe it or not I still had a little change left over to meet my friends once a week for a beer or two.

If you can stick to this habit you will suddenly start to see how the power of saving and living beneath your means can change both your mindset and your lifestyle, being frugal is not about being tight with your money but being smart with it. The next step I took was to try and reduce my debts, starting with the smallest one first.

REDUCE DEBT

I had been pretty much living off my credit cards for five or six years, sometimes paying them off completely, but usually just paying the minimum required every month. This is honestly the worst thing you can do as you are mainly just paying the interest of the debt and never the actual debt. And with credit cards the interest rates are extremely high. Credit cards are great when you need quick access to money, but it's money you don't actually own and they seriously destroy your ability to invest, save money and build wealth. Many wealthy people say that you should never spend anything on your credit card which you cannot pay off in full at the end of the month.

Make it your goal to pay off your debts, starting with the smallest one first, this could be a loan you are paying back or a credit card debt you have accumulated. Maybe the 10% you have put away each month could be increased to 15% with 5% of your income being dedicated only to debt reduction. Or maybe you have saved enough in your 10% money pot to pay off a large debt altogether. I used to pay around €500 a month to my credit cards as well as another €300 towards other debts. Now that €800 a month goes towards investments and building wealth.

Sell Anything You Do Not Need

As I have already explained I liked to buy clothes, shoes, electrical equipment, golf equipment and sometimes even expensive watches. And I was doing this even though I owed thousands of Euros to the bank and to my credit cards. The only advantage of this was I realised I had a lot of stuff I could now sell! So I went on a huge selling spree, using Facebook Marketplace, eBay and other free advertising channels. I even sent my customers a list of my golf equipment which helped me sell even more. In the end, I sold over €6,500 worth of stuff in around 3 months.

It was so refreshing: suddenly I could boost my savings pots and pay off some of my debts. Take a look around you how often do you use the PlayStation and its 30 games, the beautiful mountain bike downstairs, the hardly worn Rolex, the three sets of golf clubs in the cellar, not to mention the brand new Armani Jacket? I realised I had accumulated so many things that were simply lying around my apartment looking pretty. I even sold clothes and shoes which I never used, a stereo and microphone, and the old mobile phones that were in a cupboard collecting dust.

I do not miss anything I sold during that period, even the beautiful luxury watch, and it really helped me get rid of some of my debts and put more money into my savings account. Even if I did momentarily miss something, I knew that what I was doing would allow me to easily purchase a replacement, but without the debt hanging over my head.

Save to Invest

When you begin your mission of saving money you want to achieve two main goals. One is to have money on the side in case of emergencies or a change of employment circumstances. This is a smart idea and one I think everybody should try to achieve. But in the current environment (2021) interest rates are very low and the money you are saving in your account is not earning anything for you. The second goal is to make your money work for you and this means looking to invest your money into schemes which potentially increase its value over time, as opposed to liabilities which decrease the value of your money over time.

Investments such as stocks and shares, property, precious metals, artwork and the like have the potential to grow your money. Liabilities are actually investments that depreciate in value the longer you hold them, so your car (unless it is a very rare Ferrari) is a liability because it is costing you money to run tax and insure and its actual value is going down every year. Naturally there is always a risk associated with investments but normally it is a sensible calculated risk so long as you do not speculate or gamble your money.

If you are continually growing your money over many years, your overall wealth will increase and you will not be so reliant on your monthly income. Be diligent in the process, keep saving money and paying into your pension scheme as well as investing in other areas and you will soon see that you have accumulated a lot of money in a relatively short period of time. If you know nothing about investing, then read books about it, go to see a financial advisor or talk to people you know who have experience in investing to find the best options for you.

CREATE, DON'T CONSUME

One of the best mindsets to have is to decide you will be a creator rather than a consumer. This is a strategy I came across while reading *The Entrepreneur Revolution* by Daniel Priestley. The idea is that many of the items you currently spend your money on should actually be things you are personally creating yourself. If you invest a lot of money in books then you should write one and sell it. If you invest in courses and education then you should be selling your own courses online. If you spend money on products and services then become the creator of those products and services. This way you are creating and earning not spending and consuming.

All the information in this book has been gathered to help you maximise your income and build a successful, sustainable coaching business. But if you cannot manage your money then it really doesn't matter how much you earn. The world is full of high earners who bring in millions every year and still manage to go bankrupt. Regardless of your income you must be able to manage your money in order to build long term wealth.

SUMMARY – CHAPTER TEN

- Building wealth is about making a financial plan, being disciplined with it and understanding yourself and your spending habits
- Create different saving pots to help you divide your money up and pay yourself first
- Reduce your unnecessary spending, sell unused products and goods, cancel all luxury subscriptions, and use the money saved to save and invest in your future
- Pay off as much debt as you possibly can, starting with the smallest debts and / or change loan providers to get the very lowest interest rates possible
- Always pay yourself first, no matter what the situation is your money needs to be divided into your saving and investment pots before you pay other bills
- Try to avoid buying anything that is considered to be a liability (something that is decreasing in value the longer you keep it) the more liabilities you have the more you are throwing away money
- Consider pension plans, high interest saving accounts, stocks and shares and investments in property to build your wealth. Anything that can grow your money is a good investment
- Try to be a creator rather than a consumer, look where you like to spend your money, could you create that product or service and sell it yourself?

CONCLUSION

My mission was to write a book which would help any sports coach to develop a successful, sustainable coaching business using the methods and experiences I have gathered over my 20 years of coaching. I am by no means an expert in any of the fields mentioned in this book, and I didn't create any of these ideas from scratch. I have read and learned from the best coaches, entrepreneurs and businessmen in the world today and have tried to implement those lessons into this book and into my own coaching businesses and life, with some success.

My journey is still continuing and I work every day towards my success vision. I am constantly looking for new and creative ways in which I can add value for my customers but also increase my overall income which can then be used to build my long term wealth.

Throughout this book I have shared ideas with you that will help you change the way you work, add innovative services and products to your portfolio, build new customer bases and business partnerships, and help you work your way up to becoming a key person of influence. Running a coaching business is a great privilege, and the opportunity to help others improve their knowledge, skills and enjoyment of a sport is something that you should be truly proud of.

As you increase your knowledge and begin to find your place within your industry, it is important to appreciate every obstacle and difficulty that comes your way. An entrepreneur lives for those moments and understands that a journey like the one you are about to begin has its ups and downs and isn't always sunshine and cocktails. Make it your mission to become the best coach you can be by implementing all of the self development and business strategies in this book and you will find that maximising your income will be a very enjoyable process which will progress a lot quickly than you might have thought.

I have truly enjoyed the process of writing this book for you and I want to thank all the great coaches, teachers, mentors and entrepreneurs who I have studied and listened to for sharing their knowledge with me and helping me become a better person for it.

Go now and change your world!

Adam Lambe

Printed in Great Britain
by Amazon